Angels
Here Among Us

Angels
Here Among Us

Vernon Oickle

FOLK
LORE
PUBLISHING

The Publisher: Folklore Publishing
Website: www.folklorepublishing.com

Library and Archives Canada Cataloguing in Publication

Oickle, Vernon L.
    Angels Here Among Us / Vernon Oickle.

Includes bibliographical references.

ISBN 978-1-926677-70-5

    1. Angels. I. Title.

BL477.O53 2010   202'.15   C2010-901853-2

Project Director: Faye Boer
Project Editor: Kathy van Denderen
Front Cover Image: © iStock Photo | Luis Sandoval Mandujano
Photo Credits: Photo.com (pp. 10, 50, 83, 131, 186, 222; back cover)

We acknowledge the support of the Alberta Foundation for the Arts for our publishing program.

We acknowledge the financial support of the Government of Canada through the Book Publishing Industry Development Program (BPIDP) for our publishing activities.

Canadian Heritage
Patrimoine canadien

PC: 5

Dedicated to the memory of my own special angels:
Todd and Heather

Acknowledgments

This book would not have been possible without the support of several people, but none are more important than those who opened their hearts and bravely shared their stories. They did so because they wanted to let others know that no matter how difficult life can sometimes get, there is always hope that the situation will improve. Their message is simple—pick yourself up and hang on, as tomorrow is a new day filled with promise. I'm truly thankful to have met these wonderful individuals, and I'm honored that they have trusted me to tell their stories. It has been a humbling experience, and they have my undying gratitude.

As well, I wish to acknowledge the publisher, Faye Boer, for having sufficient faith in my abilities to greenlight this project, and to book editor Kathy van Denderen for her expert guidance. Finally, I must once again acknowledge the support and understanding of my family, who shared this journey with me. None of this would have been possible without them.

–Vernon Oickle

Contents

Introduction

The idea for this book on angels grew from my earlier work in collecting and writing ghost stories of the Maritimes. Over the years, I discovered many stories from people who had extraordinary experiences and had wonderful, inspirational messages to share. Those stories did not fit the format of my ghost books, so they largely remained unused until Folklore Publishing agreed that not only was there sufficient material to do this book but also that these stories should be shared. So began the process of researching and writing this collection.

Between these covers you will encounter people who have inspirational stories to share. While the stories may seem impossible and often too amazing to be true, they are genuine. I ask that you keep an open mind as you read.

In writing this book, I made two promises to the individuals who so bravely told of their experiences. First, that I would not judge them, because it is my job as the author simply to relate their stories, and second, that I would do everything I could to keep their identities a secret whenever they wished. In some cases, I have used pseudonyms to ensure their anonymity.

For the most part, these people have largely suffered from embarrassment and ridicule whenever they previously shared their experiences. Because of the deeply personal nature of many of their stories, these people are now reluctant to go public, but they all insist that their experiences were real. And all the individuals have two things in common: they have suffered unimaginable life-altering challenges yet they have persevered, and, although the stories are not meant to preach religion, each person encountered something that renewed their faith, be it in humanity, God or something greater than the existence we know.

PART I
In Our Darkest Hours

Someone Is Watching

PEOPLE FACING TRAUMATIC experiences will often look for answers as to why a tragedy has befallen them. Depending upon the circumstances of the incident, the answers are usually never forthcoming. When Melissa from Saint John, New Brunswick, lost her seven-year-old daughter, Megan, in a tragic motor vehicle accident several years ago, she was, naturally, heartbroken, and she searched for answers.

"I didn't think that I would get through it," she recalls, explaining that she was living in Ontario at the time.

But today, even though the loss of her daughter still breaks her heart, Melissa has found a way to cope because she knows that an angel watches over Megan.

"I know that I will never ever get over the deep, deep pain I felt when I lost my daughter," Melissa says, tears welling in her eyes and the suffering rushing to the surface, as fresh today as it was at the time of the accident. "But I truly believe she has gone to a better place.... I have to believe that. I know many people say they don't believe in the afterlife and God and heaven, but I know they exist. I've seen a glimpse of it, and I know it's real."

Parents are not supposed to outlive their children, but Melissa knows that tragedy can strike in an instant and without warning.

"I never thought that when we headed out in the car that afternoon that it would be the last time we would be together," she says, recalling the day Megan was killed in a horrific highway crash that left three dead. Two others in the second vehicle that slid across the road and into the passenger side of her car also died in the mishap.

"If you knew how your life was going to unfold, you'd plan things accordingly, but you just don't know, so you take things on faith and life just happens.... I guess maybe it's good that we don't know how our life is going to turn out, because if you did, you'd never be able to cope with that knowledge."

The weather was snowy and the road conditions were treacherous that February day when Melissa set out to work with her daughter in the backseat to be dropped off at the sitter's house. There was nothing she could have done to prevent the accident, she knows that, but it still doesn't make it any easier to accept.

"It was just one of those things that was out of my control," she says, wiping away tears as she tries hard to maintain her composure. "It just happened so fast that I didn't see the car coming, but that still doesn't mean I don't feel responsible in some way. I lost her, but they told me she didn't suffer. If there's any consolation in that, then that's what I try to hang on to. I just couldn't bear to think that she suffered in any way, but the doctors told me she died instantly from her injuries."

After the accident, Melissa went numb, and everything that happened in the days following still remains a blur.

"It's like it's all a dream, a nightmare, and some day soon I will wake from it," she says. "But it's been more than four years now and I know it was real…it was all too real, and I've lost her forever."

One of the most difficult tasks that Melissa has ever had to do in her life was to bury her little girl.

"How do you prepare for that? You don't. You just kind of sleepwalk through it and you exist, but you're not really tuned in to reality. Going to that funeral was difficult. Knowing that my little girl was in that casket just about killed me. I wanted to crawl out of my own skin and run away and hide and never come out again. I couldn't see how I was going to go on with my own life. I just wanted to die. It all seemed so unfair to me. Why had I survived and she had died?"

And although Melissa says she will never get over the void that the loss of her daughter has left in her heart, something happened that day at the funeral that has forever changed her outlook on life.

"I know people will think that I was seeing things or maybe I was so upset that I convinced myself that what I saw that day was real, but I'm telling you that it was real," Melissa says with absolute conviction. "I really don't care what people think. I know what I saw, and I know in my heart that I saw an angel that day at the cemetery during the funeral."

The incident happened just as the priest was performing the committal rites at the gravesite.

"I was upset," she states. "There is absolutely no doubt about that. I was very upset and distraught. What else would I be? We were there to bury my little girl—my baby—so yes, I was upset, but that doesn't mean I don't know what I saw."

As the priest was reading the prayer, Melissa kept her eyes glued to the casket that contained her daughter, and in an instant, she saw it.

"She was just there," Melissa says with conviction. "One minute, there was no one near the casket, the next minute there was a woman standing beside it, up near the head, and I knew right away it was an angel sent to take my baby girl home."

Describing the figure, Melissa says it was not what one would typically expect an angel to look like and nothing like depicted in books or on television.

"It was a woman, and she was very plain," she explains. "In fact, at first glance, there was nothing special about her at all. She was average height and had light-brown hair and she was wearing a light-colored, long overcoat. She didn't have wings or a halo. She wasn't glowing, and she wasn't wearing white robes, nor was she floating. She didn't look anything like what you automatically think an angel should look like.

"I have no doubt it was an angel.... No one else saw the strange woman. I asked a lot of people who were at the funeral that day and no one else saw her. How can that be? If that had been a real woman, surely someone else would have seen her, but I was the only one.... There's no way," she insists.

Besides, Melissa adds, if the woman had been real, what happened to her?

"How could she appear and disappear so quickly? If she had been a real person, I would have seen her somewhere around the graveyard. But one minute she was there and the next minute she was gone. If she wasn't an angel, then there's a woman out there who can move pretty damned fast."

Melissa is convinced that the angel came to let her know that her daughter was going to be all right. "And that helps me get through the day. I will confess that I never really considered myself to be an overly religious person, and even to this day I don't get to church as often as I should, but I take comfort in knowing that there is something beyond this world."

When You Can't Go On

SOMETIMES, WHEN LIFE THROWS you a curve ball, it may seem easier just to give up and throw in the towel. When you get to a place where you feel that you can no longer keep swinging, where you have hit rock bottom, when you feel like going to bed and pulling the covers over your head, you can either continue to wallow in your own self-despair or you can pull yourself together, face your challenges and make a conscious decision to go on. Most would find the second choice difficult to do, but as Robert Malcolm says, if you don't do it, you must consider the consequences.

"And they aren't very appealing," the middle-aged man from Nova Scotia quickly adds.

Robert concedes it isn't easy to keep going in the face of such hardships, and he confesses there can be many false starts, but perseverance is the key to survival when the going gets tough. And he should know, because Robert has encountered many ups and downs in the past decade…more downs than ups, he concedes. But one day, he finally told himself that if he didn't snap out of it, he was going to die, and he realized he was not ready to do that.

Robert's problems started in the mid-1990s when he made the first of many mistakes that he regrets but knows he can't undo.

"I was in car sales, and while I was pretty good at it and made half-decent money, I just got tired of it. After more than 20 years of selling used cars, I just didn't want to do it anymore, so I changed jobs," he explains, adding that he now wishes he had just continued to sell cars. "Maybe things would be different today, but there's no way to go back, so when you make decisions you have no choice but to live with them and push forward, but you just have to be careful that you make the right choices in the first place."

After leaving his job, Robert tried doing several different types of work, including selling life insurance, working in retail and getting a job at a call center, but he didn't like any of them, and he quickly grew to regret his decision.

"That's when my life just spiraled downward. I didn't want to go work, and I began to hate my life and question my existence. Honestly, I couldn't care less if I lived or died. Nothing mattered to me. I hit rock bottom…and I mean rock bottom."

To make matters worse, it was around the same time that his wife told him she was leaving him. She had connected with another man over the Internet, and he was coming to spend some time with her. If it worked out for them, she told Robert she planned to move to British Columbia to be with him. Thankfully, he adds, while their four-year marriage was coming to an end, they had no children to worry about.

"But we had bills. Lots of them," he says, explaining that only a year before he left his job at the car dealership, they had taken out a large mortgage to buy a big house they could not really afford, and the couple each had fairly new vehicles, which meant they had several bank loans as well as all the credit card bills.

"I will be the first to admit that we lived like royalty," Robert says with honesty. "We lived way beyond our means. I was a car salesman, and she was a secretary—granted she made pretty good money at her job, but we couldn't afford to live like we lived. There is no way that we should have gone that far into debt, but you can't blame the banks for giving you the money. You should really know what you can and can't afford, and we knew we couldn't afford to spend the kind of money that we were throwing around. But we didn't care. We wanted to pretend that we were big spenders, and it caught up to us in the end."

Robert continues, "There I was, floating between jobs that I didn't like, on the verge of bankruptcy and my wife announces she was leaving me…. Talk about being kicked when you're down and out."

He became deeply depressed.

"I began withdrawing from my family and friends," he says. "I didn't want to do anything. I didn't want to leave the house. I didn't want to talk to anyone. It was a chore just to get myself up out of bed in the morning and force myself to go to work. I hated my life, and I will admit I thought of killing myself on more than one occasion. Every time my mind started heading in that direction, I would think about how my mother would cope with the news that I had killed myself, and I knew she would take it hard, but I was close to doing it several times.

"I had even thought about driving my car into the path of an oncoming 18-wheeler, but I didn't have the guts to do it. Now, when I think about what I almost did, I think about what I would've done to the poor truck driver if I had gone through with it. I might have killed him, and for certain I would've ruined his life because he would have to live with the fact that he may have killed me and wonder what he could've done to avoid the accident, as he wouldn't have known that I had committed suicide. That would've been a terrible thing for me to do to someone else who had done nothing to me, and I can't believe that I was actually close to doing it."

On the day that his wife left town, Robert went to bed and stayed there for three days, even though he knew that he could be jeopardizing his job at the call center.

"I was already on notice because I had missed so much time lately," he explains. "They had a system where you only had three warnings, then you were out, no questions asked and no second chances. They had given me way more warnings than that, but my supervisor felt sorry for me so she gave me a second and third and fourth chance, but I knew this time around I was pushing my luck…. But I didn't care. I figured I had nothing to live for, and if I lost my job, that was just one less reason to get out of bed."

Robert knew that people were worried about him, but he could not find the strength or willpower to keep going.

"I literally gave up," he admits. "Basically, I said to hell with everything. The way I saw it, my life was coming to an end regardless of what I did, so the sooner the better from my perspective."

When Robert's wife moved, she didn't take anything with her except her personal belongings, and in doing that, she also left him with all the bills.

"I'd be lying if I said I didn't hate her for leaving me to deal with everything while she went running off with her new boyfriend," he says. "But she just packed up and left. She went back to BC with this guy, and I've only heard from her a few times since she left. I think they are still together, but I don't know for sure. I have put her behind me and moved on."

Putting his problems in the past was not easy to do, however, but in time he managed to come to grips with what his life had become.

"But I didn't do it alone," he says. "I had help along the way, but not the kind of help you might think. It wasn't from a relative, a friend, a co-worker or a doctor or anything like that.… It was with the help of an angel."

It happened early in the evening on the third day of his self-induced isolation.

"I was feeling crappy," he begins the story. "I had been in bed all day because all I wanted to do was sleep. And to be honest, I'm still not sure if I was sleeping when I first heard the voice, but if I was, I eventually woke up.… I'm sure of that."

His bedroom was dark as the curtains hadn't been opened for several days, so it was difficult to see anyone, but around seven o'clock at night, he became aware of a presence near his bed.

"I had no idea who it was. At first I thought it was my mother or one of my brothers coming to check on me as they had a key to the house, and I knew they were all worried about me, but because it was so dark, I couldn't really tell. Eventually, when the visitor spoke, it was a woman's voice. It wasn't a voice that I recognized, but, strangely, I wasn't afraid. The woman told me to get up and get out of the house. Just as plain as day, I heard this woman's voice telling me to pull myself together and get on with my life. She said I had a lot to live for and that I could not just lay there and waste away."

He adds, "Now I have to be perfectly honest that I'm not a particularly religious man, and I didn't believe in ghosts and angels and stuff like that, but I'm totally convinced that this woman was an angel, and she was encouraging me to dig deep within myself to find the courage to get over my problems. I couldn't see her, but I could clearly hear her, and she was basically telling me to smarten up, that I had a lot of life left to live and not to throw it away."

The visitor, he says, didn't remain in his room for long.

"I'm not sure it was even a minute, but what she said in that short time was enough to convince me that it was time for me to take charge of my life and to change my attitude," Robert says. "So that's what I did. I lay there for a while thinking about what this woman had said. It really didn't bother me that I didn't know who she was, but I knew she was making sense. If I was going to survive this, then I had to make changes in my life, and I had to do it soon."

It wasn't easy, Robert admits, but he forced himself to get cleaned up and face his problems. In time, and day by day, he gradually pulled himself together and turned his life around. He lost his job at the call center but eventually found his way back to car sales and is now content there. He went bankrupt and lost everything he owned, including the house and his vehicles, but that was six years ago, and today his finances are in pretty good shape.

"I'm not rich," he says with a laugh, "but I'm no longer in debt up to my eyeballs."

Most importantly, he has been with another woman for the past three-and-a-half years, and the relationship has been strong.

"She is a wonderful person," Robert beams, his smile giving away his happiness. "She knows all about my problems from the past but she doesn't care. For some reason, she likes me for who I am."

As for the strange female visitor that came to his room that evening, Robert cannot explain it.

"I have no idea who she was, but I'm certain that someone was there," he says. "But really, it doesn't matter who she was. What really matters is that she gave me the willpower to continue living, and through that visitor I learned that while life will sometimes kick you when you're already down, you do have the strength to turn it around, but you have to want to do it…. I just didn't care. I'm convinced that whoever that woman was, she was an angel sent to give me the gentle shove that I clearly needed."

I asked Robert if he thought angels exist.

"At one time in my life I would have said no way," Robert says. "But today, I know they do. Angels are as real as you and I—it's just that some of us are lucky enough to experience them and some of us aren't. I consider myself to be one of the lucky ones."

Light at the End of the Tunnel

INTO EVERYONE'S LIFE A LITTLE rain must fall, but for Sarah Brown, who was born in rural New Brunswick but now lives in Nova Scotia, there was a time a few years back when she thought she would never get out from under the dark clouds that seemed to hang over her like a heavy canopy. Until recently, she never thought much about death and dying, but now she understands that death is a part of life, and she accepts that.

"It's not like you stop and think about this stuff when you're a kid," the 25-year-old woman begins, "but eventually, life catches up to you, and when it does, it can be a rude awakening. Until I hit 20, everything was just about perfect, but for a three-year stretch, everything went way off track, and I really had no idea how I was going to go on."

It started when she learned that her closest friend in the "whole wide world" had been killed in a tragic car accident.

"I got the call from Dana's mother late one Friday night," Sarah recalls as she fights to hold back the tears. "Dana worked as a waitress in one of the local bars and had been coming home from work when another car swerved across the road and hit her head-on. They said the other driver, who only had minor injuries, had fallen asleep and came across the yellow line. They said Dana was alive when they got her out of the car, but she died on the way to the hospital, from internal injuries. Her mother was beside herself when she called, and I was devastated. I just couldn't believe it. I went numb and stayed that way for the next few days. My world was destroyed."

Sarah and Dana met in the first grade and had been close friends throughout school, and they remained friends even after they graduated and both of them went to work. Dana was planning her wedding for the coming summer, and Sarah was going to be her maid of honor. The next summer, Dana was to be Sarah's maid of honor at her own wedding. Now all those plans, hopes and dreams for the future had died with Dana, and Sarah struggled to understand how something so tragic could happen to someone so young with so much to live for.

But clearly, there weren't any answers to be found. Accidents happen, and that's all there is to it. Tragic events usually defy logic, or at least the type of logic that the average person can understand, and leave a swath of sorrow and sadness in their wake.

The next few months were difficult, especially those close to Dana's wedding date.

"I felt so bad for Dana's mother and the rest of her family, but my heart especially ached for Colin, the man she was supposed to marry," she says. "I knew them all so well. They were like my second family, and I understood they were hurting from their loss because I was also dealing with the same feelings. Dana had been a major part of my life for so many years that I didn't know how I'd be able to go on without her.… No matter how hard I tried, I just couldn't make any sense out of it."

Sarah went through several difficult months, but she was eventually able to come to grips with her best friend's death.

"I had a really hard time, and I missed her with all my heart, but time does make things better," she says, reflecting on the memory of her lost friend. "I would always have a special place in my heart for Dana, but I began to move on and face the reality of life. Besides, I knew Dana wouldn't want me to mope around. She would've told me to pick myself up and get on with my life, so I tried, and eventually, day by day, it got a little easier."

However, fate had other plans for Sarah Brown. She was just starting to get her grief under control when she suffered another devastating blow, one that nearly pushed her to near breaking.

"In the midst of all of this with Dana, we learned that my mother had pancreatic cancer and that the prognosis was not good," Sarah says. "Mom had not been feeling well for a while, and we finally convinced her to see the doctor. It turns out, there was more wrong with Mom than we could have ever imagined."

The doctors told the family to prepare for the worst because, although they couldn't predict how long Sarah's mother had to live, the type of cancer she had was usually aggressive.

"On the outset, they said she might have a year, but realistically, it would be more like six or seven months," Sarah explains. "That's difficult news to digest, and I certainly wasn't prepared for that, let alone after just dealing with the loss of my best friend."

As the reality of the news settled in, Sarah tried to help her mother deal with the disease, and that meant helping her parents make all the necessary legal and burial arrangements. She found it emotionally taxing.

But, if the situation wasn't already bad enough, there was more to come.

About two months after her mother's diagnosis, Sarah's fiancé's father dropped dead of a heart attack.

"He wasn't a sick man, really. Middle-aged, and we thought in fairly good shape, but he just went so quickly without any warning whatsoever. It just blew my mind. As you can imagine, I was just about crazy," Sarah says, adding that while Joel, her fiancé, was an emotional wreck, she was not any better.

"Again, more death and sadness in my life. What was going on? What had I done to deserve this," she says, adding that as she helped Joel deal with the loss of his father, she was also helping her mother deal with her illness. And all of this was going on while she was still grieving for her best friend.

"These were the times that I wished Dana could've been there for me," Sarah says. "She was always so much stronger than me, and I missed her so bad. I had no idea on earth how I was ever going to keep going through all of this. I just couldn't see any light at the end of the tunnel."

But sometimes, she adds, a light shines through the darkness when you aren't expecting it.

"Or at least that's how it was for me," she stresses. "In the midst of everything that was going in my life at that time,

I had no reason to think that there was a God or angels or anything like that. Honestly, my life was pure hell, and if anyone had told me all of this was part of a grand plan, I think I would've punched him in the face. Yes, I was angry.… I was really angry. Life didn't seem particularly fair to me at that moment, and it was all I could do to hold my head up."

It was a challenge, she says, adding that she had to go to the funeral of Joel's father while also that same day accompanying her mother to a hospital appointment for treatments.

"It was crazy, and I was really beside myself," she says, stressing that although she considered herself to be a logically thinking person, she now firmly believes that there are forces out there that defy explanation and logic.

"For me to say that I believe in angels or anything remotely connected to the Bible is a big step," she admits. "But I have to say that, today, based on my experiences, I'm convinced that something or someone is looking out for us."

Sarah had her change of heart the night her mother died.

"She had gotten through the first year, but it was clear she wasn't going to get much more than that," she explains. "I was in a bad way. The doctor told us that he believed the end was near and that we should all say our goodbyes. She was heavily sedated because she was in a lot of pain, and it wasn't clear what she could hear, but the doctor said she would know we were there."

One by one, Sarah's two sisters and her brother went into the hospital room and spent some time with their mother. Sarah asked if she could be the last, before her father.

"I think I just needed to build up my courage by letting the others go first, but I didn't want to go in there and say good-bye," she says. "I thought that if I delayed going in to see her, it would delay the inevitable. My mother and I were very close, and saying goodbye meant I was accepting that she was going to die. I wasn't ready for that. I know you're never prepared to lose someone close, but I really wasn't ready. I had lost Dana only a year earlier, now the idea of losing my mother was just too much for me."

Finally, however, Sarah had to accept that it was going to happen and that it was her turn to see her mother.

"Besides seeing Dana in that casket, going into that hospital room where my mother was dying was probably the hardest thing I will ever have to do," she says. "But it had to be done."

Struggling to keep her emotions under control, Sarah dug deep for the courage to force herself to do it, and somehow, she managed to enter the room where her mother was resting with hoses and tubes running from her body.

"She had fought so hard for that year and endured so much," Sarah says of her mother's fight to overcome the cancer. "But even though it was a battle she knew she couldn't win, my mother never gave up, and she maintained her dignity throughout it all. She really is my hero. I saw what it meant to fight against some seemingly insurmountable odds, but I also know that in the end, she was plain worn out. I think that when you're going through something like that, your body just says enough is enough. She just couldn't take it any more."

Entering that hospital room knowing that it would be the last time that Sarah would see her mother alive was difficult and painful.

"The emotions I was feeling at that time are beyond description," she says. "My heart was breaking, and I was being torn apart on the inside because, while I wasn't ready to say goodbye to my mother, I also knew that she was in a lot of pain, and I couldn't stand the idea of her suffering anymore. This is such a dreadful disease. People shouldn't have to go through this, but it happens every day."

Taking the chair beside the bed, Sarah didn't know what to say, so she took her mother's hand and just sat there quietly for several moments collecting her thoughts.

"Finally, I just said to her, 'Mom, I know you don't want to leave us, and we don't want you to go, but we know you're tired, and it's okay for you to go,'" Sarah recalls. "Obviously, she didn't answer, but I squeezed her hand, and after a few seconds she just slowly opened her eyes and stared off into space. She kept her eyes fixed on this one particular corner of the room and, as I looked, I swear to God that all of a sudden there was this bright light that came out of nowhere. It was amazing. It was there for a few seconds and it just shimmered. It was the purest, whitest light I have ever seen. And then it was gone. I have no idea what it was or where it came from, but I knew that the end was near. I gave Mom a kiss on the forehead and told her I loved her, then I went out and got my father so that he could have a few minutes with her before she left us."

About 15 minutes later, Sarah's father emerged from the room, crying, and told his family she was gone.

"I was upset, naturally, but after seeing that light, I was suddenly overcome with a feeling of warmth—almost relief—that she was no longer in pain," Sarah says. "I was sad and even angry that I had just lost my mother, but I'm convinced that an angel had come to ease Mom's suffering, and that made me better able to cope with my loss. It was more than a light; I know it was an angel."

Today, several years later, Sarah still misses Dana and her mother, as they left voids that nothing will ever fill.

"But that light in Mother's room was, in a sense, the light at the end of a long, dark tunnel for me," she says. She and Joel have now been married about a year and a half, and life has been going quite well for her.

"That was a very dark time for me," she says. "Three deaths in a row like that is really a lot for anyone to deal with, but I now understand that's part of life, and even though I can't explain what happened in my mother's hospital room that night, whatever it was, it prepared me to better cope with my loss. If that wasn't an angel, then I have no idea what it was."

Snow Angel

MICK PRICE, 58, KNEW THAT driving the back roads of upper New York State in the middle of January can be risky business at the best of times, but to do so in the face of a raging blizzard was pure insanity. However, he also wanted to get home and was willing to take his chances despite the potential dangers.

He had been away from home since right after the holidays, but his business trip to New York City had not gone exactly as he had hoped, with several of his deals falling flat. He wanted to return to his wife and three children. He had been gone for almost two weeks and was tired of the rat race. He longed to relax at home with his family, and it was with that thought in mind that Mick set out on his three-hour drive on a late Thursday afternoon in the middle of January 1999, despite the troubling forecasts that a Nor'easter was about to blow into the region with the possibility of record snowfalls and hurricane-force winds. Despite the warnings to stay off the roads, Mick felt he could beat the bad weather and be home safe and sound before the storm hit.

He was wrong.

About an hour into the drive on the snow-covered roads, Mick knew he had made a serious miscalculation and that he should have remained in the city until the storm had passed.

However, it was too late, because to turn back now meant he would have to drive directly back into the storm. Nearing the halfway point in his journey, he felt his only chance was to outrun the blizzard, but navigating the twisting roads of upper New York State even in the daytime and in good weather conditions is sometimes a challenge. To do so in the dark and in the middle of blinding snow was impossible.

When Mick realized he was heading for the ditch, it was too late to do anything about it. On the slippery roads, there was no way he could have corrected the skid, and before he knew it, his car fishtailed, spun around several times and turned on its side in a snowbank, trapping him inside.

"It was precisely at that moment that I knew I had made a major mistake," Mick recalls, reliving the experience where he felt totally helpless. "I was trapped…. The minute my car came to a stop, I knew I was in trouble. Here I was on a deserted stretch of road in the middle of one of the worst blizzards we'd seen in decades, and no one knew where I was."

The car was stuck in the snow, but Mick was fine, although he wasn't going anywhere. Mick's wife knew he was somewhere on the roads, but she had no way of knowing exactly where he was, and it would be impossible to dispatch emergency personnel to find him until the storm passed. To make matters worse, he couldn't get any reception on his cell phone.

He later learned that his wife spent the next day calling every contact she could think of in an effort to locate her husband. She was frantic. She had no idea where he was except that he was likely stranded somewhere between their home and New York City.

"At that time, the technology wasn't what it is today. Those hills sometimes make it impossible to get a good signal, and I guess I was just down in a gully far enough that my phone was useless to me," he says.

Thankfully, his luggage was in the trunk of his car and he was able to gain access to it through the backseat to retrieve extra clothing without going outside in the driving snow.

"To be honest, I did think about putting on a couple extra layers of clothing and then trying to walk to safety," he recalls. "I thought maybe I'd be lucky enough to meet another vehicle, but then the more I thought about it, the more I realized how stupid that was because I had not seen another vehicle in while. At least if I stayed in my car, I could keep dry, and with the extra clothing and a blanket that I always carry on the backseat, I could stay warm. No matter how desperate I felt, I knew my best chance of survival was to stay with my car."

And that's what he did…for almost 33 hours.

"It was the longest two days of my life," Mick offers, suggesting that he was an idiot for not paying attention to the weather warnings.

"It was pure stupidity on my part," he admits. "Why I thought I could outrun the storm is anyone's guess, but I'd never do it again."

Being trapped in his car as the storm raged outside was a surreal experience for Mick. There were times when the wind blew so hard that it felt like it was going to pick up his car and toss it through the air.

"It was a scary experience," he says, admitting that at times he thought he was going to die. With nothing to eat and drink except a half-eaten bag of potato chips, a bottle of Coke and a package of chewing gum, Mick says that nearing the end of his ordeal, hunger was starting to get the better of him. He tried to conserve the pop, but he longed for something warm to drink. "It was bloody cold in that car, and I would have given anything for a cup of hot coffee."

Although the car still had power, Mick resisted the urge to run the engine and heat the car for an extended length of time because he feared that the exhaust pipe might be blocked and, if so, the fumes would back up into the car's interior. His fear of succumbing to carbon monoxide poisoning was greater than his fear of freezing to death. Following a strict schedule, he ran the engine once every hour for two minutes just to warm up.

"But I will admit that didn't really make much difference," he says. "The heat from doing that didn't last long."

As the storm raged on outside and the snow piled up higher around his car, there were times when Mick feared he would never be rescued.

"My biggest fear was that with so much snow coming down, my car would get buried and they wouldn't find me until the following spring," he says with an awkward chuckle, but quickly adds that while he can now make light of the situation after 11 years, he appreciates the serious danger he was in.

"Trust me, this was no laughing matter. I was going crazy being trapped inside that car, and my mind was coming up with every possible scenario that you could imagine about how I was going to die out there. I kept thinking about my wife and my kids and kicking myself for being so stupid to think I could outdrive the storm."

It was during one of those moments of feeling fear and anxiety that Mick had an experience that changed his life forever.

"I know that when you're faced with a life-or-death predicament, your mind can sometimes play tricks on you. It's your body's way of helping you cope," he states. "But I was visited by an angel, and it was because of that visitor that I found the strength to hang on."

Mick had his experience near the end of his ordeal when he was huddled under a pile of clothes and a blanket and was just about ready to accept that maybe he wasn't going to make it.

"I know I wasn't seeing things, but all of a sudden there was this ghostly-type figure in the backseat of my car," he says, describing what he saw. "It was sort of sheer and kind of glimmering, and it was transparent. It was there, but I could see through it. It was the strangest sensation I had ever experienced."

Even though the figure didn't say anything to him, Mick felt that its presence was a message urging him to hang on.

"I just had this feeling in my gut, like something telling me to keep fighting," he explains, adding that it was like an inner voice in his head telling him not to give up. "I didn't hear anything...I just sensed it."

The image didn't last long, but it was sufficient time to impress upon him the belief that he still had something to live for.

"Definitely my family," he says. "I knew I had to get back home to them."

From then on, Mick did everything he could think of to keep his mind from wandering to dark thoughts because he knew that if he went there, he might give up.

"Thinking about getting back to my family kept me alive," he says. "I have no idea what I saw in the backseat, but whatever it was, it was enough to remind me of my wife and children, and I thank God every day that someone was looking out for me."

Mick believes that he had been stranded for around 33 hours and was nearing his breaking point.

"I was pretty cold and hungry by then," he recalls, noting that he had hours earlier finished the last of his chips. "I'll admit that if they hadn't found me soon, I don't think I would have made it because I don't think I could have hung on for much longer."

However, hang on he did, and after 33 hours trapped in a car that was stuck in a snowbank, Mick was finally rescued as snow plows began clearing the roads.

"To say I was relieved would be a very serious understatement," Mick observes. "I try not to think about what would have happened if that plow hadn't come along when it did, but I'm sure this story would not have had a happy ending."

Although Mick is certain that his visitor was not a hallucination, he admits he has no idea what he saw that day.

"Honestly, I don't know," he says. "All I know is that whatever it was gave me the strength to keep on going, and if that's not what an angel should do, then I don't know what is."

Never Say Never

Janet Mathews never thought she would ever have a normal life. After running away from home at the age of 16 and being sucked into the underworld of drugs, prostitution and violence, she had given up hope of someday having a regular job and a boyfriend who didn't beat her around every day just for kicks.

However, Janet stands proud and says, "You should never say never." Janet now has a steady, rewarding job as a personal care worker, is raising two small children and has a loving partner who totally understands the kind of life she was immersed in before finding her way out of the darkness.

And her partner knows everything about her past, including that she ran away from home to escape her abusive stepfather and alcoholic mother. He also understands that she turned to prostitution to make money just to survive.

"But he is a very forgiving and understanding man," Janet says with emotion. "In a way, he is a real angel, and I'm really blessed that he found me, but he's not the only angel I've encountered."

Not by a long shot, she adds emphatically.

"Unless you've ever had to live off the street, you can't understand what it's like to be hungry or to have no place to sleep at night," Janet explains, adding that, sadly, thousands of young people in Canada today are living the type of life she managed to escape. "I am one of the lucky ones. I know that, and I'm very, very thankful.… It's the worst kind of existence you could ever imagine. You feel worthless and dirty, like you're a nobody."

Reflecting on her life, Janet acknowledges she ended up fending for herself on the streets after dropping out of high school in grade 10 and running away from home, but she quickly adds, it beat the alternative.

"It was rough, there's no doubt about that, but it was better than staying at home and having my stepfather mess with me while my mother was too drunk to stop him," she says. Her tone underlines her resolve to survive despite some of the most difficult hardships life threw at her.

"Yes, I ran away," Janet says. "And, yes, I took money for sex and I used drugs to get high so I wouldn't have to think about what I was doing. And, yes, I'd do it again because, to me, it was the only way I could survive, and when you're living on the streets, that's the number one priority—surviving."

To her credit, though, the further Janet slipped into that dark world of depravity, the harder she fought to hang on to her sanity.

"I accepted that I had to do whatever I had to do in order to survive, but I never gave up hoping that someday I'd find a way out," she says. "But I also knew that it wouldn't be easy. I had seen too many young girls get lost in that world, and they were never able to escape. It's a tragedy, and my biggest fear was that I'd be one of those girls who would just go to the streets and get lost there.... And that nobody would even care."

And Janet did get lost there for a while, and she was trapped for almost two years until fate intervened.

"Somehow, I ended up in a shelter for homeless people, and I met a wonderful woman there who did social work and, after a while, we became friends," Janet says, with relief clearly visible on her face. "She helped me to see that no matter what I had done, I was still somebody and I was important and that I deserved to have a good life."

However, even with this support, the struggle to climb out of the gutter was not an easy one.

"Even with this wonderful woman offering to help me, it took some time for me to accept that I was worth saving," she says. "I had long given up on myself because everyone I thought I could trust had ended up treating me so bad. It took me a while to build up enough trust in anyone to turn my life over to them, and until we established that friendship, I just kept doing what I had always done."

It was after one of those drug-induced nights that Janet had her epiphany.

"I was living with this guy who had me doing some pretty bad things," she recalls, adding that her epiphany had occurred after partying "pretty hard this one night that I just passed out." She admits to using some harsh drugs that evening, and some of the details are still cloudy, but she insists that the events of that night turned her life around and set her on the road to escaping from the life of depravity in which she had been trapped.

"It was early the next morning when I came to," Janet begins. "I had been out of it for a couple of hours, and the guy I was living with was still passed out on the bed. I wasn't feeling well when I woke up, and I could tell that I was going to be sick.... It wasn't good."

Janet estimates she was in the bathroom with her head in the toilet for about 10 or 15 minutes when she heard a woman's voice.

"I was in a real bad way," she recalls, reliving the moment at which her life turned a corner and she began her ascent from the gutter. "Honestly, I was just wishing I'd hurry and die just to get it over with. I had reached the time in my life where I knew that I couldn't take it anymore. I knew something had to change, and if I was going to die, then I wanted it to just happen so I could get away from all that crap."

But just as Janet was sprawled on the bathroom floor with her head in the toilet, she heard a woman talking to her.

"I had no idea who this woman was," Janet says, adding, "At first, I thought I was losing it. But the voice was loud and clear, and it was giving me a wake-up call."

"Is this how you want to live your life, Janet?" the woman asked.

"No," Janet finally answered, wondering who the voice belonged to. But looking around, Janet could not see anyone else in the bathroom with her—not that she expected to find anyone else, as she believed she was alone in the apartment except for the man in the bedroom, and he was unconscious as far as she knew.

"Then change it," the woman told her in a forceful tone.

"I can't."

"Yes. You can," the female voice replied again.

"How?"

"You must never stop fighting for what you believe in," the woman said. "You have the power to change your world."

After that, the voice stopped, and Janet remained on the bathroom floor for a while longer, maybe another 10 or 15 minutes. Finally, she pulled herself up and took a shower, all the while this mysterious woman's words kept reverberating in her head.

"I had no idea who this woman was," Janet says, "but the words she had spoken just kept bouncing around in my head. I couldn't stop thinking about what she had said to me, and I began to wonder if it was some sort of message telling me to turn my life around."

Over the ensuing days and weeks, Janet clung to the strange conversation she had with the mysterious woman in the bathroom and, in time, she began to realize that she wanted more for her life, and she wanted off the streets.

"I wanted to go back to school and to have a good job," she says, adding that eventually she found her way back to the shelter and to the social worker who had befriended her several months earlier. With that woman's help, Janet got into a residential halfway house and enrolled in an adult educational program through which she obtained her high school diploma.

Four years later, Janet completed a personal care worker program and landed a full-time job at a seniors' facility. That was over 10 years ago, and today, she has two children and is in a steady relationship. And she has put those tumultuous earlier years behind her.

"Was it easy? Absolutely not," Janet answers her own question with emotion. "It would have been easier for me to stay there and to continue using drugs. Pulling my life back together was the hardest thing I had ever done, but I believe that anything worth doing is worth fighting for, and you should never say never. I'm proof of that."

While Janet credits her social worker and her current boyfriend for sticking with her through the tough times and for pushing her to achieve her goals, she also comes back to that morning in the bathroom when she heard the woman's voice.

"I have no idea who that woman was, but I am certain I heard the voice," Janet says. "Was it an angel? I'm really not sure, but certainly in my life it was an angel, and I will be thankful for the rest of life that whoever it was came along when she did because if she hadn't, God knows where I would have ended up…. Dead, I suspect."

When the Going Gets Tough

WE'VE ALL HEARD THE OLD adage that when the going gets tough, the tough get going. There is no better example of that than Emma Stanton. After suffering through years in an abusive relationship, she finally reached the conclusion that she had to escape her tormentor because, if she didn't, someone was going to die, and most likely that person would be her. The numbers support her conclusion.

For instance, according to Statistics Canada, on average, 182 females were killed every year in Canada between 1994 and 2003. And 198 women were victims of homicide in Canada in 2004. Of the total in 2004, 62 were victims of spousal homicide: 27 women were killed by their legally married husband, 20 by a common-law partner and 15 by a separated or divorced husband. Among the solved Canadian homicides in 2004 involving male and female victims aged 15 and older, 50 percent of all women were killed by someone with whom they had an intimate relationship, either through marriage or dating. The comparative figure for men is eight percent.

So, in light of these statistics, Emma considers herself lucky to have escaped her marriage.

But the relationship wasn't always abusive, she says, adding that by no means would she ever excuse what her husband had done to her.

"There is nothing that he could ever say to me that would make me forgive him for the hell that he put me through," she says with conviction. "But I'm just saying that we didn't start out fighting. At first he was very loving and caring. Basically, he was a real nice guy…in the beginning."

Emma began dating Ray shortly after high school. A year later they were married and promptly had a baby girl.

"That's when everything turned sour," she says, recalling the first time he hit her. "I understand that having a baby is stressful, but he didn't have to take out his frustrations on me. I thought he was a bigger man than that. I was shocked. I couldn't believe that he would do that."

To his credit, Ray never hit their daughter, but Emma feared that someday the violence might escalate to that level, and that's where she drew the line.

"I took a lot of crap from Ray, but he never laid a hand on my baby girl…let's just say that would've been the last thing he ever did," she says. "I would never let him hurt my child. I'd die first or kill him to protect her."

Thankfully, it never came to that, and Emma managed to get away from Ray before he turned his temper on their child. However, there were many times when the relationship could have ended in her death.

"I know that," she says, reflecting on her past. "He had a violent streak in him that was very unpredictable, and after the baby came, his personality just seemed to change from day to night. He was never the same again, and I don't know why because he never, ever told me he didn't want to have any kids."

Once the violence started, however, it continued to escalate both in terms of frequency and severity.

"It went from verbal insults to slapping, punching and kicking to him throwing stuff at me," Emma says, recalling a time when he threw a bottle of pickles at her while she was feeding the baby and narrowly missed her. "Luckily for me, I saw it coming and managed to get out of the way. If that would have hit me in the head, God knows what would have happened. Even worse, he could have hit the baby."

According to Statistics Canada, the majority of women who report abuse indicate that the most serious form of violence experienced was being beaten, choked or threatened with a gun or a knife.

"Ray never pulled a weapon on me, but I know he could have killed me in other ways," Emma says, adding that it's difficult to admit that the man she once loved had become a monster. "I learned the hard way what he was capable of. I honestly felt that I couldn't trust him, and finally, just before the baby's first birthday, I realized that I had to get away from him. For a while, I tried to give him the benefit of the doubt, and there were times when I honestly believed the situation would get better, but it kept getting worse."

Emma finally reached her limits. She knew she had to get out of their house one evening following an explosive argument in which Ray knocked her to the bedroom floor, sexually assaulted her and punched her around. By the time Emma came to, Ray had gone to the living room and was watching television.

Emma was hurt pretty bad, but she somehow managed to pull herself up on the bed, where she cried herself to sleep. When she awoke a few hours later by the sound of her baby in the next room, she quietly made her way down the hallway to the living room, where she found Ray sleeping in one of their big armchairs. Turning quietly, she went to the baby's room. Although her little girl was not crying, she was making a lot of noises, and Emma was curious to see what the fuss was about.

Reaching the door to the baby's room, which she always kept slightly ajar, Emma peered through the opening. She was shocked to see a woman standing over her baby's crib, but Emma knew right away that this was no ordinary woman.

"She was dressed in a long white dress and, as crazy as I know this sounds, she was kind of glowing," Emma recalls, adding, "I wasn't scared to see this woman because somehow I just knew she was there looking out for my little girl.... I just knew she was my baby's angel."

As Emma slowly opened the bedroom door, the woman just vanished before her eyes, and by the time she reached the crib, the baby was fast asleep.

"It was weird. I couldn't believe that my baby was asleep because I had just heard her, and I'm certain she was awake, but there she was just sleeping like a little princess."

At that moment, Emma knew she had to get out of the house and away from her husband.

"It just suddenly dawned on me that if anything happened to me, he'd be left with the baby, and I couldn't have that," she says. With the support of her sister and a close friend, over the next few weeks, Emma made all the necessary arrangements for her and the baby. Two weeks later, while Ray was at work, Emma packed up some clothes and other items for herself and the baby, and the two moved into the safety of a women's shelter. She was given safe haven and counseling as she began the legal process of separating from her husband.

"It wasn't easy leaving the life I knew, even though it wasn't safe," Emma recalls. The idea of taking her baby and going out on her own with little financial security and not knowing what the future held for them was a major step.

"But I also knew that it was what I was supposed to do. When I saw that woman standing beside my baby's crib, I took it as a sign. Someone was trying to tell me to think of my baby, and that's the main reason I left. She's what matters most in my life, and to think she could have been in danger makes me sick."

Without hesitation, Emma says that when she thinks of the events that transpired that night, she believes, now more than ever before, that the woman was her baby's guardian angel.

"It was a pretty powerful experience, and it changed my life…for the better," she says. "I'm totally convinced that if I had not left when I did, I might not be alive today, so in a way, I guess, the woman was also my guardian angel. I'm just so thankful that I paid attention."

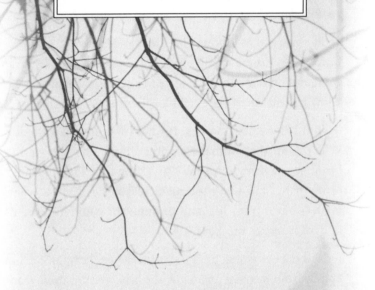

PART II
When You Need a Friend

Angel Under the Table

AT FIRST, KIMBERLY MACINTOSH didn't like to talk about her experiences because, honestly, she thought people would think she was crazy. But in the years since her encounters with her guardian angel, she has come to understand that she was not crazy at all. On the contrary, she is the sanest person she knows.

"I know it's difficult for some people to accept what I say," states the 56-year-old mother of three and grandmother of one, "but the fact is, it really happened to me, and if it wasn't for my angel, I honestly don't think that I'd be sitting here today talking about it. I really believe that people have a hard time dealing with these possibilities because, if they accept that angels and ghosts really exist, then it means there must be a greater power somewhere in the universe. A lot of people have a difficult time accepting that. But I don't. I believe it, and I believe it because of what happened to me when I was a child."

Kimberly grew up in a tumultuous home environment on the island of Cape Breton, but she does not like to reveal the location of her hometown because of the extremely personal nature of her experiences. She says her childhood was hell.

"My father was an alcoholic," she explains without hesitation. Kimberly has long ago accepted that what happened to her in her childhood was out of her control. And in a stern voice that does not betray her emotions, she quickly adds, "He was a bastard. He was cruel and mean, and there was a time that I hated the very ground that he walked on. I may have even wished he were dead."

But in time, Kimberly came to forgive her father. "I've never really forgiven him for the hell that he put me and my sister and our mom through, but I did eventually forgive him for the monster that he became because I know now that he was in a great deal of pain. He didn't work because of a back injury he suffered in a fall when he was a young man. We lived off a pension that he got and a little bit of work my mother did. He drank a lot—pretty much every day—to deal with the pain, I guess, but I still don't think that was an excuse for him to do what he did. We were his children, after all."

Her earliest memories of her childhood are of when she was six or seven years of age. "There was a time when everything just kind of become one large blur, but over the years I've been able to sort things out. I think that was part of the healing process. In order to go forward, I had to go back and put my past right in my mind. It wasn't easy, but I think it was necessary if I was going to have a normal life of any kind."

Dominating those memories was a drunken father who didn't hesitate to give her or her sister a slap or a kick if they got in his way. "It was like we were a nuisance to him. He treated our dog better than he treated his children."

However, if she and her sister were a nuisance to him, Kimberly cannot define how her father saw his wife, their mother.

"I really don't know how that woman stayed married to him for all those years. That woman was a saint, there's no doubt about that. She took a lot of crap from him, but I know now that she stayed and took it because of my sister and me. How could she leave him? Where could she go? This was at a time when women were supposed to stay with their husbands, and there wasn't a lot of support in the community for a woman on her own with two small children. It just wasn't practical. She really didn't have a life until he died. After that, she finally knew what it was like not to live in dread every day, wondering when he was going to snap and pound the living daylights out of her. I still ache for that woman, and because of that, in my own personal life, I had a difficult time warming up to a man, but thank God my marriage worked out well. I have been very fortunate that I found a wonderful man."

It didn't take much to set her father off, Kimberly recalls, remaining stoic. "In fact, he'd be fine one minute, and just like that [snapping her fingers], the next he'd be going off on you like you were his worst enemy in the world. He could turn on a dime, and it didn't matter who was around or where he was, for that matter."

Being a witness to such violence has left an indelible emotional scar on Kimberly, but she credits her survival to a special "visitor" who helped her through those dark times. Recalling when her visitor came to her for the first time, she says it was during an incident when her father was being especially brutal toward her mother, and Kimberly, just a small girl, was cowering under the kitchen table where she thought she would be safe.

"Actually, me and my sister would often hide there," Kimberly explains, fidgeting a little with her cigarette lighter.

"We didn't know what else to do, so whenever he'd explode, we'd run under the table and stay there until he calmed down. Sometimes it took hours, but we wouldn't come out until we thought it was safe.... Children shouldn't have to do that, especially in their own homes."

On this particular evening, her sister was staying at their grandparents' home, and Kimberly was home with her mother and father. "I knew it was going to be a rough one. I could sense it. You could just tell. He had been drinking all day, and you could just feel the anger building in the air. It was so thick you could cut it with a knife."

The details of the events are still clear to Kimberly because she has relived them many times in her head.

"It was August, and it was hot. I had played dolls all afternoon out on the front steps. Sissy [the name she calls her sister] was away at Nanny's house. I remember we had supper at around four o'clock and we had corn chowder. I really didn't like corn chowder all that much, but I ate it anyway because I knew better than to complain around him."

To this day, Kimberly still cannot eat corn chowder. But on that day, "We ate supper, and Mom was doing the dishes when he just went off the deep end. When I think about it, I'm not really sure what got him started, but I think it was something Mom said about needing to get school supplies for us kids and that was it. That's all it took. He just snapped."

Ranting that he didn't have money for school supplies, her father jumped up from the table like a "maniac" and began pounding her mother like she had said something really terrible to him. It really wasn't called for...." Her voice trails off.

Picking up the story again after collecting her thoughts, Kimberly states that as her parents fought, she immediately crawled under the table where she believed she would be safe. And as the confrontation escalated, the small girl remained there, crying and wishing that it would stop.

"My mother always tried to fight back and defend herself, but she was a small woman and he was a strong man," Kimberly says. "There really wasn't much she could do, but she gave it every ounce she had."

Watching the violence unfold before her eyes, Kimberly wished her sister were there with her so she wouldn't be alone. "It was bad enough when you had to watch what was happening, but it's worse when you're there alone."

About 10 minutes into the altercation, Kimberly recalls that she suddenly felt warm and "kind of fuzzy—it's hard to explain—on the inside. It was one of the most unusual and strange sensations that I have ever felt in my entire life. I just kind of tingled all over.... But it was a good feeling."

Having witnessed these fights many times in the past, Kimberly knew right away this situation was different. "The fighting was intense. There was screaming, and my mother was crying, and he was punching her, but suddenly I didn't feel alone anymore."

Perched beside her in the confined space under the kitchen table was a woman. Although Kimberly says she has difficulty defining the woman's features, she knows the visitor was female. "It sounds strange, I know, but when

I try to explain what she looked like, I can't really find the words to describe her, but I know it was a woman.... She just had womanly features, but I especially remember the long, flowing blonde hair. It reminded me of silk."

And, although Kimberly knew the woman was an adult, she still can't explain how the visitor could fit so easily under the table. "It's like, she was a full-grown adult, but somehow, she made herself fit under the table without any trouble. It's like she was my size, yet she was an adult."

In the midst of this turmoil, Kimberly immediately felt at ease and safe with this "woman" who suddenly appeared out of nowhere. "You know, I probably should have been afraid of this strange person under the table with me, but I wasn't. In fact, it was just the opposite. I stopped crying, and I felt this woman would protect me. She didn't say a word. She stayed there with me, by my side, and when the fight was over, she was gone just like that [Kimberly snaps her fingers]. I had no idea where she went or who she was, but there was no question in my mind that the woman was there."

Later that evening, as her father was sleeping, Kimberly asked her mother if she had seen the woman under the table with her, and her mother told her that she had imagined it, that the mind can play tricks on us especially when we're upset or frightened.

"But I wasn't seeing things," Kimberly insists, bristling at the idea that she could have imagined the woman. "I know what I saw. I know what I felt. There is no way that I could have imagined that."

In the years that followed the table incident, the woman came to Kimberly on many occasions, but only when she was alone. "She never showed up when my sister was around. It's like she knew that when Sissy wasn't home, I felt alone and vulnerable, and she came to be with me. And I never felt alone again."

Despite the many visits from the woman, they never spoke. "She never said a word—ever. And I never said anything to her. It's like I knew she was there to keep me safe and words were not necessary."

The last time Kimberly experienced a visit from the woman was when she was 11, and it was under similar circumstances. "When she left after that time, I just felt weird. For some reason, I knew I would never see her again, although there have been many times over the years that I wanted her to come, that I really wanted to see her."

Kimberly has absolutely no doubt that the woman was an angel sent to protect her.

"I believe that with all my heart, and even though I have not seen her for many years, I still believe she is with me every day of my life. That belief has gotten me through some very difficult times, like my mother's death." Her mother died in 2001 after fighting stomach cancer for almost two years.

After telling her mother about the visitor, Kimberly never again talked to her—or anyone else for that matter—about the woman, until years later. The first person she told was her husband, and it was he who insisted that she share her story as he thought it might help others in similar situations.

"It took me a while to build up the courage to talk about it, but finally I came to realize that he was right. Now I can talk about it without really caring what anyone else thinks. I've developed the attitude that either you believe me or you don't. But it was real. It happened."

A Helping Hand

WE ALL HAVE OUR DEMONS AND secrets, but for Rick Bedford, there was a time when his personal demons all but destroyed his life and nearly killed him in the process. Rick says without hesitation that he is a recovering alcoholic, and though he has been sober for almost seven years now, it is a daily battle. He knows that he will continue to face that challenge for the rest of his life.

Alcoholism is considered a progressive disease, meaning that the symptoms and effects of drinking alcohol become more severe over time, and Rick certainly fell into that category, as he started drinking when he was in high school. Those who use alcohol often begin slowly and some progress to showing symptoms of alcohol abuse. If the drinking continues, they may later exhibit symptoms of alcoholism or alcohol dependence. Early signs of alcoholism include frequent intoxication, and drinking and driving. Other symptoms are blackout drinking or a drastic change in demeanor while drinking, such as consistently becoming angry or violent.

Rick, now aged 54, says without hesitation that if he had not managed to get sober, he would have been dead long ago. "Either the booze would have killed me or I would have driven my car off the road and killed myself. Even worse, I may have driven my car into another vehicle and killed someone else. I could never have lived with myself if I had done something like that. Causing someone else's death by drinking and driving would be the worst thing that I could ever imagine."

Although today Rick is sober, he readily admits that he struggles with his alcoholism each and every day.

"Honesty," he says, "is the first step when dealing with this problem. You have to be honest to yourself and to those who love you. I lied to so many people for so many years that it became so bad that I didn't know what was the truth or what was fiction. It's a terrible way to live, but when you're an alcoholic, the booze controls your life and it makes you do things that you would never even think about doing if you were sober. When you're drinking as much as I was, you lose your inhibitions and you let your guard down, and I know that if I ever slip again, I will never recover. But I have promised myself that I will never allow myself to get into that state ever again…. Never."

Unfortunately, it took a near tragedy for Rick to accept the reality of his situation, and by then he had caused so much damage to himself and his family that it took years for him to get his life straightened out.

"What you have to realize is that when you're an alcoholic, you can't really control yourself," he explains. "I was an alcoholic and I didn't need a reason to drink. I had been drinking since I was about 15, and it got so bad that my body just had to have it. For the first few years, I only drank occasionally, but by the time I finished high school and then college, I was drinking almost every day. Don't ask me how I managed to get an education because, truthfully,

I have no idea as there were days that I don't even remember going to class."

Somehow, Rick managed to create a decent life for himself, getting married, having children and even building a successful career in marketing and advertising.

"Now, if you want to talk about high-pressure jobs, that would be it," Rick says, adding that the stress from his demanding career fueled his drinking problem. "But I can't blame my problems on the job. It was my fault, but the job may have been a contributing factor."

For several years, Rick drank and kept his problems hidden from everyone around him. His family knew that he enjoyed having "a few drinks," but they had no idea just how much he enjoyed it—and needed it.

"I hid it from everyone around me," he says. "Obviously, my wife knew that I drank a lot, but I always promised her that I'd quit if I thought it ever became a problem."

The real extent of that problem became evident seven years ago when he almost killed himself.

"Wow," he says, emphasizing that he can't believe just how close he came to dying the night he drove his car off the road and hit a tree. "I totaled it, but somehow I managed to walk away with hardly a scratch. It was certainly a wake-up call for me. I know it's hard to believe, but that accident was actually the best thing that could have happened to me during that period in my life. Can having a near fatal accident be good? It was for me because it forced me to take a good hard look at what I was doing, and when I did, I realized that I was living on borrowed time."

But Rick didn't reach that crossroads on his own. In fact, on the night of the accident, he had company in his car, just not the kind of company he was expecting.

"It was an angel," he insists without hesitation. "I know it sounds crazy, but I swear I encountered an angel that night just after I had the accident, and basically that's what caused me to change what I was doing to myself."

Rick was alone that fateful October night. It was raining hard and it was around nine o'clock.

"I had worked late and, yes, I did have a few drinks while I was there," he says, adding that it was normal for him to drink on the job after everyone else had left the office. "I used to think it helped the creative juices to flow, but I know now that was just an excuse to drink. I didn't get sloshed, but I certainly had more than I should have, especially since I was going to be driving home."

After completing his work for the night, Rick locked up the office, got in his car and headed home, which was about half an hour away from where he worked.

"I know I shouldn't have been behind the wheel that night," he confesses. "Besides the fact that I had been drinking…it was a miserable night weather wise. It was dark and rainy and windy, the kind of weather that made it really difficult to keep the car on the road."

In hindsight, he says, he should have pulled the car over to the road side and phoned his wife to come pick him up, but it was late, and he knew she would not want to come out in the storm.

"I could have stayed at the office," he adds, reflecting on the events. "I had done that in the past, but for whatever reason, that night I just felt like pushing the limit. So there I was, drunk behind the wheel of my car in the middle of a terrible rainstorm."

It was a recipe for tragedy.

"I was having a difficult time seeing the road," Rick says. "I think even a sober person would have had difficulty driving that night, so it was really hard for someone who had too much to drink. Maybe I was going a little fast, but I just couldn't control it."

About 15 minutes into the trip, Rick lost sight of the road, and the next thing he remembers is waking up hugging the air bag, which had deployed upon impact. He doesn't know how long he had been unconscious, but he believes it was several minutes. However, as he began to come around, he realized the seriousness of the accident.

"I was bleeding pretty hard from a bad cut to my forehead, and my chest hurt like hell from the force of the air bag, but other than that, I was okay. The car, on the other hand, was a mess," he says. "I was dazed and confused, but I could see that I had left the road and rammed headfirst into a large tree. How I avoided being killed that night is beyond me, and thank God no other vehicles were on the road or I would have hit them head-on and probably killed them and me."

As the reality of his situation set in, Rick immediately understood that he was lucky to be alive, but what happened in the next few minutes totally convinced him that he had escaped death because of divine intervention.

"Did I believe in angels before that night? No way. I always thought that stuff was a bunch of hooey, but as I struggled to get free of the seatbelt, I swear to God that I heard the voice of a woman telling me to get out. She said I didn't have much time. I heard it as plain as day. At first, I thought there was someone outside the car, but when I looked around, I couldn't see anyone. I was alone and on my own."

Instinctively, Rick knew that the car was going to catch fire and that if he didn't get out quickly, he would burn to death.

"But the seatbelt was jammed," he says with emotion as, even seven years later, his adrenaline starts to flow while he's reliving the experience. "I tried to get free, but I just couldn't budge it. Then—I swear this is true—I felt a pair of hands clasping over mine and, somehow, together we managed to force the buckle open.... But there was no one else in that car with me. I was drinking and I was dazed from the accident, but I know what I experienced, and it felt just like what an adult would do when they are helping a child. Someone helped me get out of that seatbelt and I don't know who it was, but I'm thankful someone was looking out for me."

Once free of the seatbelt, Rick pushed open the door and managed to crawl free of the wreck that had been his car. Climbing up the embankment, slippery because of the heavy rain, he made his way to safety and waited for help to arrive. Within minutes, the crumpled car burst into flames.

A subsequent investigation revealed that the car's fuel line had ruptured upon impact and a spark caused it to ignite.

"If I hadn't managed to get free, I would have been toast," Rick proclaims matter-of-factly. "When I think about how close I came to burning up in that crash, it makes me cringe. I know I was lucky to escape the full impact of the accident and I know I was lucky to get free of that seatbelt, but I'm not really sure what luck had to do with it. It's difficult to put into words how this incident affected me, but right then and there I made up my mind that I was going to stop drinking, and I did. I haven't had a single drop of alcohol since that night."

The day after the crash, inspired by his near brush with death, Rick began his recovery and eventually found Alcoholics Anonymous, where, with the support of his family and friends, he started a new life.

"Was it easy? No way," he says. "In fact, I think it was the hardest thing I have ever had to do, and it's still hard. There are times even to this day that I crave a drink, but I know that even one small drink will push me over the edge, and I'm not prepared to let that happen. I was spared that day for some reason, and I don't think it would be in my best interest to screw this up."

Not many people are given a second chance, and Rick is truly grateful that his guardian angel was looking out for him in the midst of one of the lowest times in his life. But if he falls off the wagon again, he fears that he will not be given another chance.

"I know most people don't believe me when I tell them what happened," he says. "They tell me it was the booze or the impact from the accident that caused me to have hallucinations, but I know what I experienced, and it was real. I could feel a set of hands on my hands. They were soft and as smooth as silk. For whatever reason that I can't understand, an angel was sent to help me avoid that burning wreck, and it changed my life forever. I thank God for that every day. It was a miracle, and I don't intend to mess it up."

Getting a Second Chance

SOME PEOPLE SEEM TO HAVE a difficult life, often trying to cope and succeed in the face of seemingly insurmountable circumstances over which they have little or no control.

That's exactly how it was for David Ringer, 34, who grew up in rural Nova Scotia and who readily admits to being a drug addict, an alcoholic and a thief—someone who became immersed in the world of crime and violence at a young age. He is also someone who was given a second chance, though he has no idea why he has been so fortunate.

"I broke into my first house when I was nine years old," he readily admits. He says this with such audacity that it conveys the aura of a person who believes it's okay that a young boy would commit such a crime.

But, he quickly adds, he knows it's not okay for a kid to participate in "any" illegal activity, no matter how bad life is.

"I just didn't know any better," David says. "It was very bad, and I wish I could go back and undo the damage I caused, but I can't."

David wishes he could make amends to the people he hurt through his crimes, but he knows that's not possible.

"That's the problem when you do this stuff," he says. "You hurt so many people, and you can never go back and change that. All I can do now is make sure I do what I'm supposed to do in the future because I have learned my lesson. I may have learned it the hard way, mind you, but…no matter how hard things get for me, I will never get caught in that trap again…ever."

Recalling the first theft he committed when he was nine, David knows now that it would have been best for him if he had gotten caught as it might have turned his life around. If he had been forced to face the truth right then and there, perhaps he would have made some different choices.

"But I doubt it," he admits, suggesting that he was on a path to self-destruction, and nothing could have altered that. "I had to learn my lessons the hard way. I was trouble with a capital 'T' and no one could talk to me. Believe me, a lot of people tried, but I wasn't having any of that. I may have been young, but in my mind, I knew what I was doing, and I was convinced that I'd never get caught."

And for many years he didn't.

"Breaking into that house when I was nine years old was the easiest thing I ever did, and it started me down this road to a lifetime of crime…and a lifetime of regret," he says. The house he burglarized belonged to a "nice" family in his neighborhood. "I'm not sure if they ever suspected it was me, but if they did, they never did anything about it. If it had been me, and some little brat in my neighborhood broke in and robbed my house, I'd kick his butt so hard he wouldn't be able to sit down for a week. I wouldn't have liked that much if someone had done that, but maybe it would've taught me a lesson."

David broke a window at the back of the house to gain entry and crawled in.

"It was way too easy," he recalls, adding that the sad part was that for his efforts, he left with only a little over 22 dollars in change, a few movies and, he chuckles at his naivety, a can of Pepsi.

"But the fact was, I got away with it," he says. "There was a lot more stuff there I could have taken, but I was only interested in the money. You have to remember that I was only nine, and I didn't care about most of that other stuff. They had a lot of nice items I could have stolen, but I didn't take any of it. What was I going to do with a stereo?"

However, in spite of the meager haul, his outlook as a career criminal changed in just a few short years when his drug habit forced him to steal extra money. He had to obtain the cash any way he could, and that meant he did a lot of nasty deeds he is not proud of, and most of which he would just like to forget.

"That's the worst part about being an addict," he explains, taking a long drag off his cigarette and reflecting on his past problems. "When you're an addict, you can't control your actions. The drugs control your life and make you do things you wouldn't normally do. I've known some people who have been hooked on drugs and who have done some pretty bad things, not that some of my actions would be considered nice."

Outlining some of his past indiscretions, David says he was even compelled to steal from his own family to get the money he needed to buy drugs.

"I think that's pretty much the lowest of the low," he observes. "But none of that mattered to me back then. All I cared about was getting high, and if it meant I had to take money from my family—including my poor old mother—I didn't care. All that mattered to me was getting the drugs.... I needed them. My body needed them. That's what it's like to be an addict."

By the time David reached his late teens and early 20s, he had compiled a criminal record "as long as my arm," he says.

"It ran the gamut from shoplifting, to break and enter, to theft and even assault," he readily admits. And although he is not proud of what he did, he explains that these crimes were part of who he was. "On top of that, I had a long list of charges connected to the drugs I used. There was everything from possession to trafficking, and the cops were getting pretty used to dealing with me. It's a sin, really, what I was doing with my life. I had nothing and I had no future.... I can never get those years back. It was such a waste."

David continued his criminal ways until he was almost 30, at which time he had what many people would describe as an epiphany.

"I don't know any fancy words for it or anything like that, but something strange happened to me, and whatever it was, it changed my life forever," he says, explaining that his experience occurred one weekend when he was spending time in jail.

"They had arrested me for being drunk and fighting in a public place," he recalls. "And I was.... I was loaded and I was high. When I got like that, no one could talk to me, and all I ever wanted to do was fight. I'd fight with anyone who got in my way. People I knew. People I didn't know. It didn't matter to me. When I was stoned or drunk, I'd take on the world. I'm a scrawny guy, and I've been in some major scraps, so you can just imagine how I usually came out of it. That night, when they arrested me, I was in pretty bad shape."

Because David was already on probation owing to previous convictions and was under court orders not to consume alcohol or to associate with anyone with a criminal record, he was automatically arrested and taken back to jail. As this altercation occurred on a Saturday night, he had to remain in jail through the rest of the weekend and go before a judge the following Monday.

"But you know what? Jail wasn't all that bad. It was kind of like a second home for me, and in the condition I was in that night, that's really the best thing that could have happened to me," he observes, admitting that if he hadn't ended up in jail, he might have gotten into even more trouble. It was smart to keep him away from other people because all he wanted to do was fight.

David immediately passed out when they put him into the jail cell, and he believes he was "out of it" for a couple of hours when he was awoken by a voice. As he started to come around, he could hear a man's voice talking to him.

"Are you okay?" the man asked.

At first, David could barely hear the stranger as his voice was very soft.

"Are you okay?" the man asked again.

David sat up, but when he looked around to see who was in the jail cell with him and who was talking to him, he quickly discovered he was alone.

"I thought I was cracking up," he says. "I know what I heard, and I know I heard a man's voice."

But where had the voice come from?

When the man spoke again, David realized the voice was coming from another cell.

"Are you all right?" the man asked yet again.

"Not really," David answered. "My head's pounding."

"I'm not surprised," the man responded. "You consumed a large amount alcohol this evening, and you ended up getting in a fight. So it's no wonder that you don't feel well."

"Yeah, well, he had it coming to him," David answered.

"Did he?" the man replied.

"Yes," David said. "As a matter of fact, yes, he did. That guy's always looking for trouble."

"And you?" the man answered. "Aren't you always looking for trouble?"

"I don't know what you mean," David replied, not prepared to accept responsibility for his actions.

"Sure you do, David," the man continued. David was surprised that the stranger knew his name.

"Who are you?" David asked because he was unable to see the next cell as it was around a corner.

"I'm your friend," the man answered.

"Do I know you?" David asked. "What's your name? You sound really familiar to me, like I really know you."

"Let's just say that I'm your friend, David," the man said. "I've known you a long time."

"That ain't hardly right," David answered. "You seem to know me, so why won't you tell me who you are?"

"That's not important, David," the man replied. "What's important is what I want to say to you."

"Well, I ain't listening if you don't tell me your name," David snapped.

"Yes, you will," the man answered. "There's nowhere for you to go, so you will listen."

"I ain't gonna listen," David insisted.

"You will, David, because what I have to say to you is very important," answered the unnamed man.

"What's so important that you won't tell me who you are?" David asked.

"I just want to tell you, David, that if you don't stop what you're doing, you will be dead by this time next year," the man said.

"What the hell kind of bull is that?" David snapped. "That's nothing new. People have been telling me that for a long time."

"Yes, they have, David, but you won't listen," the man continued. "But I'm telling you that if you don't stop drinking and doing drugs and fighting, you will be dead within 12 months."

And at that, the man stopped talking to David.

For the remainder of the night, David tried to sleep, but the stranger's message kept coming back to him, and he kept hearing it over and over in his head.... It haunted him like nothing ever had in the past.

"I couldn't really explain it, but I knew there was something about that man," David says. "There was just something about the way he talked that was different.... I just felt it, and it made me uncomfortable."

The next morning when the guard came to check on him, David asked about the man in the next cell around the corner. The guard looked stunned.

"What man?" the guard asked.

When David said that he was talking about the man who was in the other cell around the corner, the guard's answer left him speechless.

"David," the guard said, "there's no one in that cell. Actually, you were the only one in our cells last night.... You're the only one here."

"You're kidding, right?" David said, thinking the guard was trying to pull a fast one on him. "You're pulling my leg, aren't you?"

"No, David," the guard insisted. "There's no one else in here. I'm not sure who you were talking to last night, but it wasn't anyone in these cells."

After the guard left, David thought about the conversation he had with the stranger, and while he admits it is possible that he may have still been feeling the effects of the drugs and alcohol, he is 100 percent certain that it had taken place.

"I wasn't totally drunk, if that's what you think," David insists. "But I can't explain it, either."

Since that night, David has replayed that conversation many times in his head, and each time, he remains convinced that the incident was real.

"I know I didn't imagine it," he says. "I'm certain of that. I can't explain it, but it was real."

Who or what that man was remains a mystery to him, but David did take heed of the message.

"He told me that if I didn't change my ways, I would be dead in a year's time," David says. "And eventually I came to take that message to heart. I've tried really hard to change how I live."

But, he adds, it isn't always easy.

"Changing an entire lifetime of bad habits is hard to do, especially when your body craves certain things," he says. "And I've had many setbacks, but whenever I get in a bad way, I think of the message that man had for me and I pull myself out of it."

It has been a few years now since that night he spent in jail, and thankfully, David says, he has lived past the first anniversary.

"I have no idea what happened that night, and honestly, I've stopped trying to figure it out," David says, lighting another cigarette and taking the smoke deep into his lungs. "For some reason that I really don't understand,

I was given a second chance, and I've tried to make the most of it. I live better now than I did for 30 years so I'm working hard on it."

Does he believe that man in the other jail cell was an angel?

"I honestly don't know," David answers, reflecting on the conversation. "But something definitely weird happened that night, something that I can't explain that changed my life for the better, so yes, maybe it was an angel.... maybe that's exactly what it was."

The Man in the Doorway

Do ANGELS REALLY EXIST? THE ANSWER to that question depends upon your personal beliefs, perspective on life and emotional state. And people have been asking that question for generations, but few have ever found the answer.

However, if you ask 86-year-old Gertrude Farmer—or "Gertie" as her friends and family call her—if angels exist, she will tell you most emphatically that, yes, without a doubt, angels are real, and we are lucky to share our world with them.

Gertie believes that angels are real because she saw an angel, not once, but twice in her lifetime, and she considers herself most fortunate to have done so.

She was five years old when she saw her first angel.

"That was a long time ago," she says with a laugh. "But I remember it just as plain as if it had happened yesterday. Seeing something like that leaves a lasting memory."

It was on the occasion of her uncle's funeral, and Gertie remembers that she was with her grandmother at the church.

"It was early spring in April 1929," Gertie says. The stock market had crashed on Wall Street, plunging the world into the Great Depression; the first Academy Awards ceremony was held in Hollywood, with the movie Wings winning the award for best movie; and the Boston

Bruins had won the National Hockey League's coveted trophy, the Stanley Cup, for the first time in the history of the storied sports franchise.

"They were hard times, different times," she says. "But they were good times when people worked hard just to earn a living and when families were really close."

Now, all these years later, Gertie has nothing left of that time but memories, and she is thankful that her mind is as sharp today as it was eight decades ago.

"My memory is still as clear as ever," she says. "Everything else is giving out, but I remember that evening in April very well. It was warm, and there was a light rain, the kind of dampness that clings to the body and goes through you right to your bones, and there was fog in the air…thick fog, and it was very depressing."

Gertie's uncle Jimmy, her mother's oldest brother, went to sea on the fishing boats when he was just a young boy.

"In those days, the boys usually didn't finish school," she says, reflecting on a time long since passed. "They often had to go to work to earn a few cents to help the family pay the bills. It was tough going, but somehow people managed, and I think we were the better for it. People today are too soft. The good life has made them lazy."

It was only a few weeks after Gertie's fifth birthday that word arrived that Jimmy had been swept overboard by a rogue wave and was missing at sea. Four days later, the boat made port with the dreadful news that despite searching for two days, the crew couldn't locate Jimmy's body, and after the second day, the captain had declared him lost as there was no hope of him surviving in the north Atlantic Ocean for more than a few hours, if at all.

"It was a bad time," Gertie recalls. "My grandmother was heartbroken, but she went about making preparations for a burial just the same. Even though they didn't have a body, Nanna still insisted that she wanted a proper burial for him, so three days later, we all went to the church for the service."

It was after the service when Gertie came face to face with her first angel.

"Everyone else had gone outside. Nanna and me were the last to leave," she says. "We left the church through a side door and made our way along an old stone footpath to the front of the church.... It was there that I saw him for the first time."

As she and her grandmother passed the front entrance of the historical church with its large stone pillars and concrete steps, Gertie glanced toward the large wooden doors.

"And there he was," Gertie says with enthusiasm. "When I looked up at the doors, I noticed a man standing there. He was dressed in white and had dark hair.... He wasn't anyone I recognized, but I waved at him just the same, and when I did, Nanna asked me who I was waving to. When I told her I was waving at the man by the doors, she stopped in her tracks and looked down at me. Then she glanced back to the doors and then down at me again.... 'There is no one there, Gertie,' Nanna said to me.... But there was. I could still see him, and he smiled back at me."

Gertie insisted to her grandmother that a man was stand-ing by the doors, but the grieving woman asserted that her granddaughter was mistaken and that it must be the mist or something else that was playing tricks on her eyes.

"Nanna never did believe me that I had seen a man that evening," Gertie continues. "But I did see him, and I was immediately convinced that he was no ordinary man. He had to be an angel. Why else could I see him and not Nanna?"

No matter how many times the two discussed that incident over the years, Gertie could never convince her grandmother that the man was real.

"I think she really believed that, as a child, I had no idea what I was talking about," Gertie says. "It always bothered me that Nanna wouldn't believe me. I loved my grandmother very much, and I would never make up something like that, and I'd certainly never do it at my uncle's funeral. But she would never admit that I had seen something. Right up to the day she died, she never let on that she believed me. Perhaps she didn't or perhaps it was just too difficult to accept that something like that could actually be real."

But even if her grandmother could not believe, Gertie certainly did, and some 40 years later, she encountered her second angel.

"Nana had long since died by this time, but I couldn't help but think of her when I saw the man again," Gertie says, explaining that on this occasion she was attending another funeral at the same church. This time it was a funeral for a woman she had known since her childhood.

"Virginia and I had grown up together and we stayed friends our whole life," Gertie says. "I was heartbroken when Jenny died. That's what we called her. Jenny and I had played together as children in this town, and we raised our own families here. We were very close friends. When she got sick and we found out she had bowel cancer, it was hard for me. I didn't want to lose the best friend I had ever had, but a year after she got sick, she died, and I was a mess."

On the afternoon of Jenny's funeral, Gertie was making her way into the church when she caught a glimpse of a dark-haired man dressed in a white suit lingering around the large wooden doors at the stately entrance to the church.

"I got cold chills right away," Gertie says, shivering as the memories of that day flash through her mind. "Now I can't say that it was the same man I had seen over 40 years earlier, but it certainly looked like him. It looked so much like him that it was really uncanny…. And if it was the same man, he hadn't aged a day."

Gertie's husband had accompanied her to Jenny's funeral and, noticing that she had suddenly become overly anxious, asked Gertie if she was okay. She replied that she was not okay, and she quickly related the stories about her two sightings of this mysterious man.

Glancing toward the wooden doors, her husband promptly informed her that he could not see a man dressed in white. In fact, he told her that no one was at the entrance because most of the people were already inside the church and had taken their seats as the service was about to begin.

"But it didn't matter to me what my husband said," Gertie says. "I know what I saw, and it was a man, and he was at the church doors just like the first time I had seen him."

Gertie admits that it bothers her that neither her grandmother nor her husband believed that she had experienced
something extraordinary at the church, and she accepts that
some people have difficulty accepting the unexplainable.
But she believes that she had seen an angel on both of those
occasions.

"I know that some people can't believe that angels and
ghosts exist, but I believe," she says. "I have faith that there's
more to this life than what we know here on earth. I believe
that some people are more tuned in to that other world than
others…"

Gertie considers herself blessed to have witnessed such
a miracle twice in her lifetime, and she thinks that makes
her special.

"Most people go through their entire life and never
experience anything like that, not even once, but I've done it
twice," she says. "I consider myself to have been very lucky."

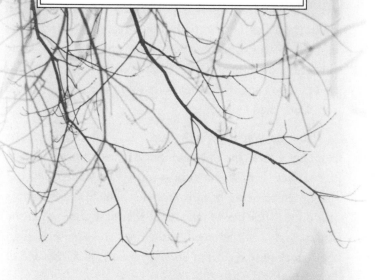

PART III
Through the Eyes of a Child

You Are My Sunshine

THE ABSOLUTE WORST FEAR FOR parents is that their child will get sick, and for parents who hear the difficult news that their child has a potentially life-threatening disease, it's as if their world has crashed down around them. That's certainly how Lisa and Tim Warner from Nova Scotia felt several years ago when they were told their three-year-old son, Cody, had leukemia.

"How do you cope with that?" Lisa asks, wiping tears from her eyes as the raw emotions of those times bubble to the surface. It has been almost four years since Cody was diagnosed as being in full remission, but Lisa admits it is still difficult for her to talk about that dark time when she almost lost her little boy. But she does so because, though their story may seem sad and depressing, it is also one of inspiration and faith.

"It's the worst nightmare you could ever imagine for a parent," she says. "When the doctor sits across his desk from you and tells you that your little boy has that awful disease, you just go numb. Really, you just don't know what to do or say or what to feel. You cry and you fear for the worst, but you also hang onto any small shred of hope that your child will beat this."

When Cody began experiencing fevers and ear infections, the family doctor sent him for routine blood tests, but at first nothing showed up. But when the little boy became extremely tired for no obvious reason, stopped eating and complained that his arms and legs hurt, the doctor told Lisa and Tim that he felt Cody should have more tests—there had to be some reason for his persistent problems.

"He wouldn't speculate or offer any theories so, of course, by this time, we were starting to think the worst," Lisa continues. "Whenever your children aren't feeling well, you automatically think there's something seriously wrong, and I could tell Cody was really sick. Call it a mother's intuition, but I just had this feeling in my heart that something was really wrong with him. I knew the longer it took to do these tests, the worse he could get. I wanted answers, and I wanted them fast."

They got an answer, and it was the most difficult news she has ever had to hear. The doctors told Lisa and Tim that Cody had leukemia, but fortunately, it was a type that could be cured if treatment was started right away. Naturally, the couple immediately agreed to do whatever had to be done to help Cody.

"I would have given up my own life if it would have helped Cody in a way," Lisa asserts, insisting that any mother would make a similar sacrifice. "The idea that my little boy was facing this terrible ordeal was really hard for me to face, but I knew I had to be strong for him. I couldn't help him if I fell apart. I took a leave from my job, but Tim had to keep working, so that meant I was the one that would be going through this with Cody, and that meant I had to keep smiling even when it was tearing my heart out."

The term "leukemia" refers to cancers of the white blood cells, and the disease can be fatal. Doctors explained to Lisa and Tim that in leukemia, large numbers of abnormal white blood cells are produced in the bone marrow. These white cells crowd the bone marrow and flood the bloodstream, but they cannot perform their proper role of protecting the body against disease because they are defective.

As leukemia progresses, the cancer interferes with the body's production of other types of blood cells, including red blood cells and platelets. This results in anemia, or low numbers of red cells, and bleeding problems, in addition to the increased risk of infection caused by white blood cell abnormalities. Fortunately, the doctors also told Lisa and Tim that the chances for a cure were very good and that with treatment, most children with leukemia live their lives free of the disease without it coming back.

"Of course we went through all the steps you go through when you're handed this type of news," Lisa explains. "Why him? We were sad and we denied it at first. Then we became angry that of all the children out there, Cody had to be the one to get sick, but that was really selfish of us. We know it happens to a lot of children, as we met many sick children during this journey, many of them in more serious shape than Cody. After the anger, we just became resigned to the reality that we were given this problem for whatever reason, and once we accepted the facts, we committed ourselves to helping Cody through this terrible ordeal."

And, she adds through tears, it wasn't easy.

"It was hard," Lisa says. "It was very hard. Seeing my child suffering for hours at a time and being in a lot of pain was the most difficult thing I ever had to do. I would have changed places with him in heartbeat. If I could have taken on that pain for him, I would have, and I prayed to God every day for Him to make it stop."

Although the treatments were often painful and usually made Cody sick, Lisa understood that the process was making him better at the same time, and she remained supportive of his treatment.

"It's just that when you're in that moment, you see the situation as it is right then," she says. "And I knew he was suffering. The doctors and nurses were really good with him, and they tried to do whatever they could to make him comfortable. We couldn't have asked for any better care than we received. If there are real angels out there, then the men and women who work in that hospital were certainly angels."

But as caring as the medical staff was, Lisa is convinced that Cody had another kind of special angel looking out for him.

"I didn't see her myself," Lisa admits, "but Cody says he saw her many times, and he talked to her, too. Now I know I'm talking about taking the word of a sick little boy who was often sedated, but something special happened to him in that hospital room while he was receiving treatment, and it was something that I can't explain."

These days, when a child is admitted for treatment, hospitals require that at least one parent remain with the child. There was no question that Lisa would be staying with Cody.

"The staff was really helpful and kind," she says. "They walked us through this and prepared us as best they could, but it was difficult leaving our home, and although Tim would often visit, he couldn't stay over so we missed him a lot. Cody really missed his dad, but the reality was that Tim had to keep working. It's just a fact of life."

It's an ordeal to be confined to a hospital room, and Lisa says there were times, late at night, while Cody was sleeping, that she'd take a break and go to the cafeteria or patients' lounge just to get some time for herself.

"I was never gone long, and the nurses always knew how to reach me if something happened. They give you a pager when you leave the floor so that they can always be in touch in case something comes up and they need you," she says. "I didn't leave his room the first few nights, but the nurses encourage you to leave to take a break. They've seen enough to know that if you don't give yourself some room to breathe, then you'll crack under the pressure, and that wasn't going to help my son, they'd tell me."

On night four, Lisa finally decided to take the nurses' advice.

"He was sound asleep when I left the room and sleeping very comfortably," she explains. "I don't think I was gone any more than 30 minutes, just long enough to get a cup of tea and to watch the late-night news. When I got back to the room, Cody was awake. At first I thought there was some-thing wrong. I asked him if he was okay or if he felt sick, and he told me, no, he felt good. I told him he should then try to go back to sleep because he needed to rest as the medicine works better when he's sleeping."

What happened next left Lisa speechless.

"He asked me if I could sing him the song again. I asked him what song, and he told me he liked the song that I was just singing to him. It made him feel happy."

Because Lisa had just returned to the room, she had no idea what her son was talking about so she asked him to tell her about it, and she thought that maybe he had been dreaming.

"'You know the words, Mommy,' he said to me. Then he started singing, 'You are my sunshine, my only sunshine,' and I just about freaked out," Lisa continues. "I hadn't heard that song since I was a little child and my grand-mother used to sing it to me. I know for certain that I had never sang it to Cody and, in fact, I hadn't thought of that song in many years."

Her initial reaction was one of disbelief, but then she concluded that maybe one of the nurses had been in to check on Cody and had sang it to him. Telling her son that she would be right back, Lisa went out to the nurses' station to talk with the duty nurse.

"They assured me that since Cody was hooked up to monitors and that because he was sleeping well when I left him, there had been no reason for any of them to be in his room," she says. "They told me that no one had been in there since I had left…but someone was."

Returning to Cody, Lisa tried asking him a few more questions about the song and who had sung it to him, but he was too tired to reply and quickly fell asleep.

Over the next few days, Lisa eventually forgot about the song incident until Cody started singing it again. This time, she pressed him for details.

"When I asked him where he heard that song, he told me the woman sang it to him," she says. "When I asked him what woman, he told me the woman who comes into his room every time I leave. I asked him to describe the woman to me and he said she was just a woman but that she was really nice and fun, and she sang that song to him every time she visited."

Lisa can't explain where he got the idea that the woman visited him because she never saw anyone in his room, other than family, and whenever she asked the nurses about it, they said they had no idea who Cody was talking about.

"I thought it might have been one of those volunteers who come into the hospitals to give parents a break," she says. "I had seen some of those women around the hospital, but I never met any of them. The nurses told me that if I ever needed a break, they would ask one of the volunteers to come by and stay with Cody, but I never asked so, honestly, I have no idea who this woman was, but whoever she was, she was certainly making Cody feel good.... He loved that song. He only knew the first two lines of it, but he sang it all the time, and if that was going to make him happy, then I wasn't going to question him about it."

Lisa does not know how many times this woman visited Cody when he was in the hospital because after a while she stopped asking him about the visitor.

"He seemed like he was doing really well, and the doctors were saying it looked like his condition was improving, so I figured why rock the boat? If these visits from this strange woman were in any way contributing to his prognosis, then I wasn't about to complain about it," she says, adding, "Besides, I wouldn't know who to complain to since the hospital insisted that the woman had no connection to the staff."

In total, Cody was in and out of the hospital for about a year before he finally got a clean bill of health. Over time, the frequency of his visits to get checked out was cut back. Today, he is required to make only one visit per year for testing.

"They will keep doing that for a while to make sure the cancer hasn't come back, but as of right now, they tell us he is cancer free," Lisa says, the tears returning as she is overcome with relief and happiness. "Unless you have gone through something like this with your own child, there is no way you can know how that feels. It's the best news we could ever hope for."

Today, Cody is a happy little boy who shows no lasting effects from the leukemia or the treatments, and the doctors have told Lisa and Tim that if he makes it five years without the cancer returning, then he'll have a good chance of having a normal life.

"But we'll always worry about him," she says. "We'll always live with the fear that it might come back. I think that's only natural, but Tim and I have both promised that we are not going to let this control our lives. Cody will know what we went through, but we are not going to dwell on it.... For now, it's one day at a time."

As for Cody's visitor, Lisa has no idea who this woman was, and she has stopped asking him about it.

"I've let it drop," she says. "He went through so much during that time that I don't want to keep reminding him of it. He still sings the song every now and then, but he doesn't talk about it.... But I certainly have theories as to who she was. I'm convinced that the woman who visited Cody was an angel. I'm certain of that. I've thought about this since he was sick, and that's the only explanation I can come up with. Who else was this woman? Besides, the fact that she sang him a song that my grandmother used to sing to me when I was a kid was just too much of a coincidence. If this woman's presence allowed him to cope with what he was going through, then I'm just thankful that she came to him. Whoever she was, she was certainly an angel in my book."

A Hero Is As a Hero Does

ELEVEN-YEAR-OLD AARON RICHARDSON doesn't consider himself a hero, but to his family, that's exactly what he is, and the facts of his story support their claim. Furthermore, if actions define a hero, then he deserves the title.

Around 2008, Aaron rescued his parents, his brother and his sister from what could have been a terrible tragedy. Instead, it ended with a celebration of courage and a renewed sense of faith for all those involved.

Aaron's story begins when he was nine, and by his parents' description, their son was just your average child—a good student who got along with everyone he met and who loved to play street hockey with the kids in his neighborhood.

"That was his only passion," his father, Steve, says. "He loves hockey. He loves playing it, and he loves watching it on television. Now, for me, I'm not into the sport, but I support him whenever I can."

"I swear he practically sleeps and eats hockey," adds his mother, Amy, explaining that Aaron is outside with his hockey stick when he gets up in the morning and before he comes into the house at night. "I'm not really sure where his love for the game comes from, because neither me or his father are particularly fond of hockey. We'll watch the games with him, but not because we like it, but because he gets so much pleasure from it. I'd rather watch a good movie, but our Saturday evenings are usually spent watching a game."

Aaron's favorite team is the Toronto Maple Leafs, and when asked why, he answers with pride and enthusiasm, "Just because."

Although hockey obviously plays an important role in Aaron's life, this story isn't about Canada's national pastime. In fact, the only connection this story has to hockey is that it takes place on a Saturday when the family had gone to bed after watching a hockey game on television—the Leafs lost again, Aaron states with the appreciative and supportive grin of a diehard fan.

Steve explains that based on the timeline that they were able to put together, it appears as though the chain of events started shortly before 3:00 AM, probably around 2:45 or 2:50.

"It's all a bit sketchy," Amy adds, as she hugs her young-est child and gives him a kiss on the cheek. "It all seemed to happen so quickly that at first it was just a blur, but after everything settled down and we had the chance to assess what happened, we think we've been able to piece it all together."

Steve and Amy have long ago given up trying to figure out what happened in their son's room that November night. Instead, they have decided to accept it without ques-tion because sometimes events happen for which there is no simple answer.

Aaron picks up the story and, even though he admits he was sound asleep when everything started, he insists that he knows what he saw.

"Yup," he says without hesitation. "It wasn't a dream."

Aaron is the first to admit that when he's sleeping, he's usually hard to wake up. Both parents nod in agreement.

"I sometimes joke with Mom and Dad that the house could fall down around me when I'm sleeping and I wouldn't hear anything," Aaron says. However, on this particular night, it wasn't so much the house falling down that woke him from his deep sleep.

"Like I said, I was sound asleep," he says with an air of confidence that suggests he is more mature than one would expect from an 11-year-old boy. "I don't really remember what woke me up, but something did. I remember I just kind of had this weird feeling. It was kind of like a dream but not really a dream…. It's hard to explain.

"Anyway, I just woke up," he says. "And when I did, I had this weird feeling that somebody else was in the room with me. I couldn't see anyone because it was really dark, but it felt like someone was there. At first, I thought it was Mom or Dad. And I remember thinking that I wasn't scared or anything like that."

But when Aaron called out for his parents and no one answered, he thought it strange that he couldn't see whoever was there in his room.

"Then, after a while, I started getting scared," he admits. "I didn't know what was going on, but I knew something wasn't right."

Instead of getting out of bed, Aaron continued to lie there, wondering who was in his room and what the person wanted.

"It was really dark and I didn't know what I should do," he says, adding that he has no idea how long he lay there before he felt the bed move for the first time.

"It just shook a little," he says. "Not really hard, but just kind of easy, almost as if someone was trying to get me to move or something like that. It was kind of like how you would shake the bed if you were trying to get someone to wake up.

"It freaked me out, and I was starting to get pretty scared by this time. I couldn't see anyone, so it was freaking me out that my bed was moving like that."

When he called out again for his parents and no one came, Aaron decided that maybe he should get up and go tell his mother and father what was taking place in his room.

As Aaron pushed the covers back and put his feet on the floor, the bed stopped moving.

"Then I really started freaking out," he says, adding that he quickly made his way to his bedroom door. All the bedrooms were on the second level, and when Aaron opened the door to his room, he was not prepared for what greeted him.

"It [the upstairs hallway] was full of smoke," he says as memories of what happened next flood his brain. "There was smoke everywhere, and it was so thick that I couldn't see where I was going."

That's when instinct kicked in, and Aaron knew he had to get everyone up and out of the house. He didn't know where the fire was, but he could tell it must be bad.

Because his brother's room was next to his, Aaron woke Trevor first. Together, the boys woke Hillary, their sister, and then, because their parents' room was at the end of the hallway, Aaron ran to their door and woke them.

"It was worse than I could ever imagine," Steve says, recalling his stunned surprise when his son shook him awake. "You're never prepared for something like that. I didn't know what was going on, but when I realized what Aaron was saying, I told Amy to get up, that there was a fire and that we needed to get out of the house."

"The first thing you think about is the children," Amy adds, noting that the smoke was so thick in their bedroom that she didn't even realize that Aaron was standing beside the bed and had been the one to sound the alarm. "I'm not really sure I knew what was going on, but Steve and I were sleeping through the smoke alarm. It might have had something to do with the amount of smoke in our room, I don't know, but neither of us had heard it going off…. If it hadn't been for Aaron, I don't even want to think about what could have happened."

Making sure his parents were both out of bed, Aaron led them down the hallway to the stairs and then out the front door.

"He was so amazing," Amy says, brushing the light-brown hair on his head. "He remained so calm through it all and helped get us all out of the burning house. He's certainly our hero."

"He certainly is," Steve says, echoing his wife's pride in the courage displayed by their young son in the face of a possible tragedy. "That was a brave thing he did."

No question, but after the family came to grips with losing their home and most of their possessions, they asked Aaron about the events of that night.

In the beginning, Aaron wouldn't tell his parents what had happened. He thought they wouldn't believe him, but Amy says they would have.

"Why wouldn't we? Obviously something was going on in his room that night, and just because we don't understand it doesn't mean it didn't happen. If he says someone was there, then I believe him."

"And," Steve says, "once he started telling us about his visitor, the details of his story remain consistent no matter how many times he tells it, which tells us that he certainly believes in what he is saying.... Did an angel come to Aaron's room and wake him up that night so that he could save us from dying in that fire? I don't know, but something definitely happened because if it hadn't been for him, there's no way of knowing how this would have ended."

But if Steve seems somewhat reluctant to accept that divine intervention played a role in Aaron's actions, Amy has no hesitation whatsoever.

"I absolutely believe it was an angel who came and woke him up. How else do you explain the presence in his room and the bed shaking? Something stepped in that night and saved us, and it had to be an angel. What else could it have been?" she says.

For his part, Aaron isn't sure if he believes that some divine being rescued him. In fact, he doesn't like to think about it.

"If I admit that angels exist, then does that mean other bad things exist?" he asks.

Good question.

Although Aaron knows that something was in his room that night, and whatever it was woke him up, he has no idea what it was.

"I didn't see anything," he says. "It was too dark in my room and it was too smoky in the hallway to see anything."

Regardless, Amy and Steve say they are thankful that Aaron kept his head when he woke up and realized something was wrong.

"He could have so easily panicked," Steve says, adding that the reaction would have been perfectly understandable. "But he stayed focused, and because of that we were able to get out without anyone being harmed, and that's all that matters. He's a hero in our books."

Following a subsequent investigation, it was determined that the fire started in the kitchen as the result of an electrical shortage.

"We were lucky," Steve says, shaking his head. "We were very lucky."

And Baby Makes Three

WHEN DOCTORS TOLD SHERRY AND Darcy Matthews that they were going to have a baby, the couple, who live in a Boston suburb, were ecstatic. After trying for nearly a decade to conceive, they had all but given up hope of ever having a baby of their own. However, in the spring of 2002, while going through the lengthy adoption process, the couple received the blessed news that despite the odds, Sherry was indeed pregnant, and the pair considered it a miracle.

"It had been a painful process, but after years of tests, we had gotten ourselves to the place where we had accepted the fact that we wouldn't be able to have our own child," Sherry says, recalling the pain of having to hear such a prognosis. "But despite what all the doctors said, somehow a miracle happened and we were able to conceive. We just considered ourselves to be so very blessed that despite everything we had been through, it was finally going to happen for us. It's really impossible to put into words how we felt, but I never questioned it; I just accepted that it was meant to be."

Considering the odds that were stacked against them and in light of all the complications the couple had endured over the years, Sherry's doctor cautioned her and Darcy about becoming too attached to their unborn baby, encouraging them to be happy but also to be prepared for the worst possible outcome.

"They felt that because of our medical history and the problems we had in the past, it might be impossible for me to carry the baby full term," Sherry recalls. "So even though it was hard to control our excitement, we tried to take the pregnancy one day at a time, and we prayed every step of the way."

With the doctors carefully watching her progress, Sherry counted the months, and each day she became more hopeful that she was going to carry the baby to full term.

"We were so happy," she says, "but even though we prepared to welcome our new baby, we resisted the urge to let ourselves become so caught up in the possibilities, both good and bad. We went day-by-day, but I will admit that it became more and more difficult for us not to throw ourselves into this pregnancy."

However, after five months—the longest Sherry had ever carried a baby—the happy couple could no longer hold back their emotions or excitement.

"We had been waiting for this for so long that we just threw ourselves into our new baby with all of our hearts and souls," she says. "We always knew in the back of our minds that there was a chance that something could go wrong, but we just couldn't contain ourselves. Just imagine how hard that would be after trying to have a baby for more than 10 years."

With each day that went by and with each positive check-up with the doctors, the Matthews grew more and more hopeful that they were finally going to be parents. However, the day after the end of her second trimester, Sherry awoke early in the morning with severe cramping pains and immediately noticed that she was spotting, both signs that something was seriously wrong with the pregnancy.

"I was freaking out," she says, recalling that she woke Darcy and told him to call the hospital. They were instructed to bring Sherry to the hospital. Following a series of tests, it was determined that the baby was in great distress. Even though there didn't seem to be any clear reason for the problems, doctors told the distraught couple that the fetus had turned in the uterus and was now presenting in a breech position, but the bigger threat to both the mother and baby was the loss of blood. Considering Sherry's medical history, along with the other factors now in play, doctors recommended that although the baby would be three months prema-ture, it should be delivered immediately to prevent further complications. A cesarean section was quickly scheduled.

"Honestly," Sherry says, "I'm not sure I was 100 percent convinced that was best for the baby, but we had no choice but to trust the doctors. They had gotten us this far, so we put our faith in them to save our baby."

Although Sherry admits to never really thinking about God, she prayed that her baby would survive the delivery.

"I just couldn't have taken another disappointment if anything had happened to my baby," she says. "It just wouldn't have been good. I'm not sure how I would have survived another disappointment after having carried the baby further than any of the others in the past."

As preparations continued for the surgery, Sherry became more distraught while thinking about the health of her unborn child.

"I wasn't in good shape," she states, and when the procedure finally began, she became very emotional. "I was a wreck, and I had Darcy worked into a lather as well. I knew he was worrying about the baby, but he was also concerned about me."

During a cesarean section, the expectant mother is awake and totally conscious of what's happening around her in the operating room.

"I could see and hear everything," Sherry says, adding, "I really don't think all of that confusion and activity was helping me much. It's bad enough knowing what they were doing, but being able to see the doctors and nurses hurrying around in their masks and hearing them talk was making me worry even more, and because I was awake, I wanted to know everything that was happening with the baby. Thank God Darcy was in there with me."

As the medical staff scurried about making final preparations for the surgery, Sherry tried to do her best to remain calm, but she was having a difficult time keeping her emotions in check.

"I just kept asking why this was happening," she recalls as the memories force tears to the surface, the emotions still fresh after all this time. "I couldn't understand why this was happening to us. Why couldn't we have a baby like everyone else? Had I done something in the past that I was now being punished for?"

Despite the emotions and stress, however, Sherry has clear memories of what was happening in the operating room.

"I was aware of everything and I was very lucid," she insists, adding that's why when she had her unusual vision she knew it wasn't in her imagination.

"I was very upset," she states, "but I know what I saw, and whatever it was, it made me relax, because in that one split second, I knew everything was going to be okay."

Sherry explains that as the doctor began to make his incision, "this huge, bright light" suddenly engulfed him.

"I have no idea where it came from, but it made me feel warm all over," she says. "I asked Darcy if he saw the light, but he couldn't see it.... But it was there.... It really was."

Other than Sherry, no one else in the room could see the light. Regardless, though, the warm glow immediately had a calming effect on her. As she began to relax, Sherry was certain that in the light she could see the outline of a woman, who was standing directly behind the doctor as if she was looking over his shoulder and watching what he was doing.

"In that very moment, I stopped worrying," Sherry says. "I knew everything was going to be just fine and that my baby was going to be okay."

Fifteen minutes after the surgery began, Sherry and Darcy welcomed their new daughter, Sophie Grace, into the world.

"It was a miracle," Sherry observes. "Even though she was early, she was just a perfect little girl.... I was so happy to finally be able to hold her. All my prayers were answered that day, and now I believe that angels do watch over us. I know Darcy thinks I was just so emotional that I was see-ing things, but I know what I saw, and I know there was a light and a woman there that day.... She was my angel, and she was there to make sure Sophie found her way to us."

After a two-week stay in the hospital, Sophie was welcomed home by her proud parents. Today, Sophie Grace is a happy and healthy eight-year-old little girl who takes piano lessons and enjoys gymnastics and swimming.

"She is everything we could have imagined," Sherry says. "For some reason, we were given this miracle child and we have enjoyed every minute of every day with her."

But the Matthews' story does not end there. Two months after Sherry and Darcy welcomed baby Sophie Grace into their loving home, they received notification that their adoption application had been approved. And three months after that, the couple welcomed a second baby girl, Amber, into their home. Today Sherry says the girls are as close as if they were biologically connected.

"It's just so beautiful how they have bonded and grown up with each other," Sherry says. "When Amber came into our home and hearts, our family was completed. I do believe in angels, and I have two little angels right in my own home. As for the other type of angels, I believe in them as well, because I have seen one with my own eyes."

Pushing the Limit

WHEN IT COMES TO THE HUMAN SPIRIT, there really is no way to measure just how far a person can be pushed before breaking. However, there are many recorded accounts of those who go well beyond most expectations, even in the face of seemingly impossible odds. Such is the case of Rebecca Evans, a nine-year-old girl who found a hidden reserve of strength and courage that she never knew she had.

Becca, as her friends and family know her, admits that she had broken the rules and ultimately put herself in harm's way. But she also learned her lesson and in the process discovered something important about herself and the world around her: you never know what you can do until you are actually pushed.

The five members of the Evans family, from New Brunswick, are avid campers who spend almost the entire summer exploring the great outdoors. Cathy, Becca's mom, says they all enjoy horseback riding, hiking and other summer sports, but especially swimming.

"Our three children were swimming long before they could walk," Cathy says, a distinct hint of pride sparkling in her eye. "We had a strong belief that if they were going to learn one thing then it was going to be how to respect the water, because we thought that could someday save their lives. That was important to my husband and me. Becca and her sister and brother are all excellent swimmers, and in the summer they spend a lot of time in the water. I'm surprised they haven't grown gills after all these years."

But Cathy also understands that even the best and most experienced swimmers can run into trouble.

"You have to respect the water," she observes. "That's really the bottom line. The minute you think you're better than the water, that's the minute you're in trouble because the water will always win in the end."

And that's exactly what happened to Becca.

In the summer of 2007, the Evans family was touring Nova Scotia's campgrounds and having a good time until near tragedy struck.

"It was a horrifying experience, and I will never forget how I felt that day when I realized that Becca was in trouble," Cathy says, explaining that no matter how experienced the children were at swimming or how many people were around the lakeshore, she or her husband always accompanied the children to the water. "It's not that we didn't trust the children. It's just that we know how quickly things can happen and, besides, we enjoyed going with them. Even if we didn't always go in the water ourselves, we still liked to sit on the shore and watch them."

This day, Cathy volunteered to take the children to the water so that her husband could finish setting up the campsite. It was late afternoon, and she planned to take the children swimming for an hour or so and then make supper when she returned to camp.

"We had been to this particular campground on several occasions in the past and we liked it there," Cathy says. "We like swimming in pools well enough, but we also like fresh-water lakes. There's just something refreshing about swimming in water without a bunch of chlorine or chemicals, and we all prefer fresh water to the ocean. It's warmer and there's no sand, which I hate, but that's just me."

The children were having a great time playing and splashing around in the water. Instead of joining them, Cathy chose to sit in the shade of several trees that stood near the lake's edge.

"It just seemed like a normal day. The kids were having a good time doing what they enjoy the most, and I was relaxing with a good book. What could go wrong?"

Plenty.

Becca picks up the story.

"I wasn't really trying to be smart or anything like that," says the young girl with such honesty that it is impossible not to believe her. "I was just swimming with my brother and sister and we were having lots of fun. But then…"

She pauses as if asking her mother for permission to continue the story. Cathy nods for her carry on.

"…then I think I got carried away," Becca says, explaining that before she knew it, she had swum way out into the deep water. "I knew I wasn't supposed to be that far out from shore, but for some reason that day I just wanted to see how far I could go."

She has no idea what possessed her to push the limit.

"I just did," she admits, then quickly adds, "I went way too far out."

By the time Cathy glanced up from her book and realized that Becca was nowhere near her brother and sister where she was supposed to be, the little girl was out in the middle of the lake.

"Naturally, I panicked," Cathy says, admitting that she yelled for her daughter to come in right away. "Even though I knew Becca was a strong swimmer, I also knew that she couldn't handle that deep water, especially if she became fatigued."

"But I didn't hear her," Becca says, adding that by the time she had noticed how far out in the lake she had gone, she was in big trouble. "And I don't mean with Mom. I was in trouble because I was really, really tired, and I realized that I wouldn't be able to get back in to shore."

Becca immediately froze.

"I couldn't hear Mom, and I couldn't even see her on the shore," Becca says. "That's how far out in the lake I was."

Instinctively, she began treading water, but her arms and legs were getting tired, and she was getting scared.

"I tried to make my arms and legs go," she says, "but they wouldn't move. They felt really, really heavy."

Although Becca doesn't think she panicked when she realized her predicament, she admits that she didn't know what to do.

"I started to cry," she says. "I had been swimming long enough to know that if you get tired and you're that far out in deep water, then you might drown..... I didn't want to drown."

Both Becca and Cathy are unsure how long the girl was out there.

"I'd say it was at least 10 minutes, because she was out there a good distance," Cathy says, explaining that her first instinct was to jump into the water and swim toward her daughter. "I told the other kids to be quick and go get their dad, and I swam as fast as I could toward Becca, but she was out there quite a distance, so I feared I wouldn't reach her in time."

All the while, Cathy kept scolding herself for not paying closer attention to the children.

"Naturally, I take a lot of the blame myself," she says. "I was the adult. I was the parent. I should have been watching them more closely. Instead, I was reading a book.... That will never happen again."

"But Mom," Becca jumps in. "It wasn't your fault. I'm the one who went way out in the lake, even though I knew I wasn't supposed to."

Regardless of who was to blame, both mother and daughter agree that Becca had been in serious trouble.

"I tried telling myself that I had to move," Becca says, as an involuntary shiver betrays the emotions she feels while reliving her near brush with death, "but I was just too tired, and all I wanted to do was rest."

Becca felt her eyes closing. If that had happened, she knows it would have been too late for her.

But then she heard "this voice," even though no one was near her, and it was telling her not to give up.

"This voice told me to move my arms and my legs. She said, 'Come on, Rebecca. You have to move. You can do it, Rebecca. Do not give up,'" she says, repeating the words from this mysterious voice. "I heard the voice a couple of times telling me to swim toward Mom and then, all of a sudden, I just felt my arms and legs starting to move and before I knew it, I was swimming toward the shore."

Becca still didn't see her mother swimming toward her, but she insists that the voice she heard was not her mom's.

"I think I would know what my mother's voice would sound like," Becca says. "It wasn't Mom…. This voice kept pushing me and saying stuff like, 'That's good, Rebecca. Keep going, Rebecca. Kick your feet, Rebecca.' She never called me 'Becca' like everyone else."

A few minutes later, when Cathy finally reached her daughter, she could see that Becca was exhausted.

"She was really tired, and I knew that if I had not gotten to her when I did, then it would have been too late," Cathy explains, adding that she is positive that her daughter would have drowned that afternoon. "I was terrified but relieved at the same time that I had reached her when I did, because another few minutes later and who knows what would have happened."

For her part, Becca was so tired that she really doesn't remember swimming into the waiting arms of her mother… but she remembers the voice.

"I do," she says with enthusiasm. "I remember the voice. It was a woman, and she was friendly, and she told me not to give up, that I could make it but I had to kick my legs and move my arms. She kept telling me to move, and I did."

If there had been another woman out in the lake that afternoon, Cathy is convinced that she would have seen her.

"But I can tell you with 100 percent certainty that there was absolutely no one else out there in that water that afternoon. I'm positive about that," she insists, pausing to consider the alternatives. "Where would she have gone? If there was no one else out there, yet Becca insists she heard a voice encouraging her to swim, then who was it…or what was it?"

There's one other thing that has nagged Cathy since Becca told her about the woman—how did she know the little girl's name?

Cathy's husband tells her that if another person was in the lake that day, it's possible she would have heard the children calling Becca by her name.

"But I don't buy that," Cathy says. "We hardly ever use her given name, and certainly her brother and sister would never call her Rebecca. We all call her Becca, yet this mysterious woman called her Rebecca. That's just too weird for me."

But regardless how it happened, Cathy is just relieved that the situation ended as it did.

"For whatever reason, Becca found a way to push herself beyond the limit," she says, thankful that a family tragedy appeared to have been miraculously averted. "I've been around water all my life and I know how quickly accidents can happen. It was scary for a few minutes, but it could have been a whole lot worse for us."

Becca now knows that when her mom and dad set boundaries, they do so for a reason, and even though she may not fully understand them, she promises she will never disobey them.

"I won't do that again," she insists with the youthful exuberance of a child who has learned an important lesson, albeit the hard way.

The White People

BILLY GARDNER'S STORY STARTS ONE COLD Saturday in January several years ago when he accompanied his older brother, Patrick, and two other boys from their neighborhood to a nearby lake where the kids often played shinny hockey throughout the winter. Most years, the lake doesn't freeze until after Christmas, but that year the cold weather seemed to grip the region several weeks earlier than usual, and by mid-December all the kids in the neighborhood were skating on the lake. However, an unseasonably mild stretch near the end of January contributed to an early thaw and, unbeknownst to the children, the ice became unstable and unsafe, setting the stage for a story of heroism and survival.

And that is where Billy, Patrick and the two other boys come in.

After lunch that January day, the boys gathered their hockey gear and headed down to the lake for a game. They loved hockey and usually spent several hours there every Saturday and Sunday. The plan was for the Gardner boys to take on their two neighborhood rivals in a friendly game with bragging rights up for grabs, a powerful motivator for young competitive players such as these boys.

It was an exciting defensive game, with both sides doing extremely well at keeping their opponents at bay.

Around three o'clock, the boys decided to take a break before playing some more. While Patrick and the others rested at a clearing on the side of the lake, seven-year-old Billy, still full of energy and feeling especially hyper that afternoon, chose instead to skate around the lake in an ever-widening circle. Billy loved to skate and he was good at it, and even though Patrick had warned him to avoid the black patches as it meant the ice was thin there, Billy felt he was quick enough to escape any cracks should they occur.

He was wrong.

While skating near the center of the lake, Billy suddenly felt the ice give way under him, and before he realized what was happening, he felt himself sliding feet first into the frigid water. As he struggled to hold on to the ice, the weight of his skates and winter clothing pulled him downward and, although putting up a valiant struggle, within minutes Billy gave in to the numbing cold of the water and slipped out of sight under the ice.

Thankfully, Patrick had been watching his younger brother from his resting place on shore and saw what had happened. Telling one of the other boys to go get help, Patrick and the second friend skated toward the opening where they had last seen Billy. However, by the time they reached the hole, the younger Gardner boy was nowhere to be seen. The only sign of Billy was his hockey stick laying on the ice where he had dropped it before plunging into the cold water.

Within short order, the boys' parents arrived at the lake, followed a few minutes later by rescue personnel from the local fire department and the police. As word spread that one of the Gardner boys had fallen through the ice, curious and concerned onlookers gathered on the shore. Everyone knew there was a very small window of survival in such frigid waters, and they braced for the worst. Rescuers, who had experience with these types of emergencies, knew that time was of the essence. Quickly springing into action, they lowered ropes into the opening, hoping that if Billy was still near the hole and was still clinging to the ice, he might see the ropes and grab on, or so everyone prayed. A second hole was cut into the ice farther down the lake, directly in the path that the current was flowing. As well, divers were immediately summoned to the scene, and within half an hour, two men in wet suits entered the freezing water looking for Billy.

With each minute that passed, hope that Billy would be found alive grew dimmer, but as the day's light started to fade, the divers finally located him farther downstream. He had been beneath the ice for two hours. Considering the amount of time that had elapsed, it was doubtful that Billy would survive in such extreme temperatures. Paramedics went to work on the small boy, and within minutes they announced that although he was in dire shape, they could detect a very weak pulse. They cautioned, however, that there could be many reasons for this faint heartbeat, but at least he had a chance. Billy required immediate medical attention.

Normal body temperature is around 98.6°F, as measured in the mouth. Hypothermia is defined as a drop in body temperature below 95°F. When the body becomes very cold, all physiological systems begin to slow down, which can eventually threaten survival. In some rare cases, though, hypothermia can save lives. There are documented cases where children who have fallen into freezing water have been successfully revived even when they have no heartbeat. Their below-normal temperature slowed down their brain function and caused their bodies to use less oxygen, thus extending their chances of survival.

Treatment of hypothermia needs to be done carefully and under proper supervision, as in this state, the body is extremely fragile. Medical personnel will slowly warm up the body with heating pads, packs and special blankets while administering warmed intravenous fluids and oxygen. They also monitor the patient for any heart problems and give the proper medications if needed. Even if the patient has no pulse, doctors still go ahead with re-warming the patient as well as applying cardio-pulmonary resuscitation.

Billy's condition was critical, and the doctors told the Gardners that even though many people have recovered after severe hypothermia, more often than not the victim succumbs to the cold temperatures. However, because Billy had a slight pulse, it was a positive sign that there might be a slim chance, and the doctors assured Billy's parents they would do everything they could to help him.

"We prayed," Billy's mom, Wanda, recalls, as she relives those tense hours. "We prayed for a miracle, and it was touch and go for several hours as doctors worked to keep him alive and to bring him out of his frozen state. They told us that they had to do it very slowly because if they warmed him up too quickly, it might put his body into shock.... They were the most difficult hours I have ever had to endure."

Finally, 12 hours after Billy had fallen through the ice, he began to shows signs of progress. It would take several more days before doctors could tell if any of his organs had suffered permanent damage, but following an initial examination, it looked as though Billy was going to pull through.

"It was a miracle," Wanda declares, adding that in the days that followed, the family became convinced that Billy had survived because of an act of God. The doctors told Wanda and her husband that all their tests indicated Billy would make a complete recovery, and five days later he was brought home.

Once Billy was home, he began telling a story that made his parents believe that more had been at play that day down at the lake than just first responders and emergency personnel, all heroes in their own right.

Medicine played a major role in Billy's recovery, but his parents also believe angels saved Billy that day.

Why?

Because Billy told them a story that no seven-year-old child should be able to recount so well.

"When he told us the story," Wanda explains, "he told it in a way that was just too grown for a child. He used words after the accident that he had never used before, and he told the story in such great detail that we couldn't believe that it was him talking. Billy has always been a smart boy, but this was way beyond his abilities."

Three days after he returned home from the hospital, Billy told his mom about his experience under the ice. Wanda was getting him ready for bed when he blurted out the story.

"He said, 'You know, Mommy, the White People helped me that day under the ice.' I wasn't sure what he was talking about so I pressed him for details. I asked him what he meant, and he said, 'After I fell through the ice, the White People came and got me. They put their arms around me and kept me warm and safe. They carried me downstream and stayed with me until the firemen found me.'"

Wanda admits that at first she dismissed Billy's story as nothing more than the words of a confused child who was suffering from the effects of a traumatic brush with death. She asked Billy what they looked like and what they were wearing.

"He told me they looked like birds because they had wings, and they were all white, and there were three or four of them. He was so sure of what he had seen that when he spoke, I got the feeling I should believe him. Then he said, 'The White People helped me to get to the hole in the ice where the firemen were, and they told me that it was time for me go back.'"

When Wanda asked her son what he thought they meant by that, he replied, "They told me to go back and tell everyone about the White People."

"He also told me the White People had told him that he should not be afraid and that he would see his mommy and daddy and Patrick again," Wanda says.

Considering the ordeal Billy had undergone, Wanda wasn't surprised her son may have imagined that he had seen these "White People," and at first she told him that it was a dream.

"But he insisted they were real. He said, 'No, Mommy. They want you to believe that they are real. They want me to tell people they are here and that they are all around us. They are here to help us.' I wasn't sure how I felt about having my son going around telling people about what he says happened to him that day under the ice, but honestly, I wasn't sure what I should do. I wasn't sure if it was good to encourage him or to try to convince him that he had only imagined these things, but the truth is, I could tell he really believed what he was saying. I didn't want to do anything that would harm his recovery."

In the end, Wanda decided not to discourage him. Instead, she checked with the family doctor to get his opinion.

"Naturally, the doctors dismissed his visions as a result of the trauma he had suffered," Wanda says. "They said we had to understand that when the body is forced into these extreme conditions, it will react and start shutting down, and when that happens, the mind can play tricks on us. We really have no way of knowing what that would do to Billy's brain, so the doctors said it is likely that he was hallucinating when he saw these White People and maybe he was…but I just don't know. To hear Billy talk about them, you'd think they were as real as you and me. He insists that they were there that day and that they rescued him."

The truth is, Wanda actually believes her son.

"And it's not just as simple as a mother believing her child's fanciful story," she adds. "It's more than that. I've seen his face and felt his emotions when he talks about how these White People kept him safe that day. He really believes it."

And, she adds, "Who's to say he didn't have this experience? We saw a lot of miracles that day, and maybe there was more there than we could see with our own eyes. Maybe Billy saw something that only a few select groups of people get to see. Maybe he was one of the lucky ones. Why shouldn't we believe him?"

Where There's Smoke

OFTENTIMES WHEN PEOPLE ARE IN extremely stressful situations, especially if their life may be in danger, their eyes can play tricks on them, leading them to believe they have seen something even when they know that is not possible. But other times, even against such logic, such manifestations are too real to ignore.

That's exactly how it was for 10-year-old Danny, who insists that he survived a tragic house fire because someone—or something—was there to protect him. And his grandmother, Sheila, agrees that whatever happened that March night several years ago had such a profound and lasting effect on the boy that she has no doubt something extraordinary occurred. However, she quickly adds, because Danny is the only surviving witness to the events, no one can confirm what he says happened either before or after the fire.

For legal and emotional reasons, Sheila insists that their identities remain anonymous. Her grandson and other members of her family have already suffered enough pain and tragedy, and she doesn't want to subject Danny to any further grief. However, Danny's story is extraordinary, so she allows him to talk about it. In a way, she believes it might be therapeutic for him to get it out in the open. She fears that keeping his thoughts and feelings bottled up inside might only do him more harm.

While details of what transpired in that house during that early March evening remain sketchy, events culminated with a tragic fire that left all the members of Danny's immediate family dead, including his parents, his sister and an uncle. And if not for some sort of divine intervention, Sheila believes that her grandson would also have been killed.

Sheila explains that it was no secret Danny's household was a troubled one. She accepts that her son had a drug and alcohol problem and that when he was under the influence of these substances, he became a totally different person with an extreme temper highlighted by a streak of violence that always worried her.

"He had a short fuse," she states candidly, readily admitting that she witnessed him explode on more than a few occasions. "He always had a bad temper, even as a child, but when he was drinking, he became three times worse. He could change on a dime. When he was sober, he was a great guy, but when he was drunk, even I will admit that he was not fit to be around because he could be fine one minute, joking and being a real nice guy, but he could turn on you in a second, and you didn't have to give him a reason. He just snapped."

And when her son went into one of those temper flare-ups, it was best to avoid him.

"Even if he was being an ass, we knew better than to confront him," she says, adding that she and her husband learned early on not to get up in his face. "He just wouldn't back down, and he'd fight no matter how big you were or if he knew you or not. Didn't matter to him if you were a perfect stranger, he'd jump at the chance to fight. He was a scrappy little cuss, there is no doubt about that."

Unfortunately, Sheila's daughter-in-law, Danny's mother, was a lot like her son, and when the two of them squared off, it was like throwing gasoline on a fire.

"It wasn't a good environment for children," Sheila says in reflecting upon the household in which her grandchildren were living. "My husband and I tried to keep watch over them, but there was only so much we could do. They weren't our children so we had limited rights. Believe me, if there was a way we could have gotten those children away from that house—away from their parents, especially their father—we would have done it in a heartbeat. But that just wasn't going to happen.… Their mother was very defensive and protective that way, and she hated us interfering."

Sheila wishes she would have fought harder for the children and that maybe if she had taken her concerns to the proper authorities, there might have been a different outcome.

"But he was our son, and no matter how bad you know things are, no parent ever wants to see their child in trouble, so we did the best we could," she says. "But clearly it wasn't enough. Believe me, I live with those regrets every day, and if I could go back and do it over, I'd do so in a second, but we try to make the most of it, and even though we regret what happened, we're thankful that we have Danny."

When details emerged about the events that transpired in Danny's household that evening, Sheila says she cried for days thinking that she had let her grandchildren down, and now one of them is dead and the other may be scarred for the rest of his life. But she has hope for Danny's future well-being because of the story he tells about a special visitor he had that night, a visitor who helped him and protected him until help arrived.

As Danny tells the story, he remembers that his mother and father had been fighting for most of the day.

"They were arguing a lot," he says. "And they were yelling at each other.… I hated it when they fought like that. When they fought, me and my sister would go to our rooms and play video games. Sometimes we'd play together and some-times we went to our own rooms, but it didn't matter where we went, we knew we had to get away from them."

On the evening of the fire, Danny heard his parents quarrel for hours, and he could tell that his father was getting angrier.

"He just wouldn't let it drop," Danny says, "and I knew Mommy wasn't going to stop either, so they just kept fight-ing and yelling. It was so bad that I had to turn up the sound on my game so I could hear it over them."

When asked, Danny says he has no idea what his parents were fighting over.

"They argued all the time," he says. "Just about every day."

Eventually, during his parents' escalating argument, he fell asleep while lying on top of the covers. He doesn't recall what time he dosed off, and he doesn't know how long he had been sleeping.

But when Danny finally woke up, he was surprised to notice that the house was completely silent.

"I couldn't hear a sound," he says, explaining that instead of getting up, he continued to lay on his bed in the darkness, listening for his parents and wondering what had happened to everyone. A few minutes later, he caught the first whiff of smoke.

"I didn't know what it was at first," he says, but then the smell kept getting stronger and stronger. "It burned my nose so I knew it must be a fire." Danny began to panic and wondered what he should do.

"I was afraid," he admits. "I wanted Mom to come and get me, but she didn't."

As the smell of the smoke grew stronger, Danny began to realize that he should get out of the house because he could tell by the amount of smoke that the fire was pretty bad, and it was getting worse.

"But I didn't know what to do," he says. He continued to sit on his bed, trying to figure out why his mother wasn't coming for him and wondering which way he should go.

Danny thinks he sat there for a couple of minutes when suddenly his bedroom door flew open and he could see the smoke and fire outside in the hallway. He knew he couldn't get out of the house by going into the hallway. But how? He was frightened and cried out for help.

As he stared out into the hallway at the flames, he was suddenly surprised to feel another presence with him in the bedroom. He says it was a woman, and she was dressed in white. Danny didn't know who she was, but he says she spoke to him.

"She said, 'Come with me.' And I did," Danny says, adding that even though this woman was a stranger, he suddenly felt safe with her.

Quickly joining the mysterious woman near his bedroom door, Danny says she reached out and took his hand and told him not to be afraid because she was there to help him.

"So I took her hand and we went out into the hallway," Danny says. "There was flames and fire all around us and lots of smoke. I could see that we couldn't get down the stairway because it was blocked by the fire."

Instead of heading into the fire, the woman led Danny into the bathroom, closed the door and told him to get into the bathtub and to lie down. "She told me to stay there and that she would stay with me until someone came to help."

Danny has no idea how long he was in the bathroom before he heard the firefighters coming through the door, but however long it was, the mysterious woman remained with him, standing near the bathtub and telling him not to worry because the men would soon be there to rescue him.

But he knows he was there for several minutes, and then finally, he heard a firefighter calling out for anyone who might still be in the house. Danny yelled out that he was in the bathroom, and it was then that he noticed the woman had disappeared. He didn't see her go.

"She stayed with me until the firemen came, but then she was gone," he says, adding again that he has no idea who she was, and she never told him her name. "But she was very nice. I liked her."

By the time Sheila heard about the fire, it was too late. Rushing to the scene, she and her husband found the two-storey structure fully engulfed in flames, and the fire was already shooting out through the roof.

"We prayed that everyone was all right, but we weren't there but for a few minutes when a police officer told us we should expect the worst because there was word from the inside that there were casualties," Sheila recalls, her emotions rushing to the surface as she relives that tragic night. At that time, she still had no idea who was alive or if, in fact, anyone was.

"It was hard," she says, "standing there watching that house burn and not knowing if anyone had survived."

Finally, after many excruciatingly long minutes, a police officer broke the news that following an initial search of the house, firefighters found the bodies of two adult males, one adult female and one child, but they had rescued a boy and he appeared to be unharmed.

Sheila knew that based on what the officer had just told them, her son, his wife, his wife's brother and Sheila's grand-daughter were gone, but as that reality gripped her, she also knew she had to be strong for Danny. She was told that paramedics were putting Danny into an ambulance and he would be taken to the hospital for evaluation, but he appeared to be fine other than being a little confused and shaken up.

Following the ambulance to the hospital, Sheila says neither she nor her husband said a word about the tragedy that was now embracing their family.

"We had just had some devastating news, and while both of us were broken up by it, I think we were both surprised that this hadn't happened sooner," she freely confesses. "But regardless of what had happened in that house that night, I knew it was now our job to take care of Danny, and that's what we've been doing. We've welcomed him into our home with open arms. He is such a wonderful young man."

As part of the investigation into the fire, police interviewed Danny several times, and he repeated the same details each time—his parents had been fighting, he fell asleep in his room playing video games, he had no idea how long he was sleeping, he woke up and smelled smoke and he stayed in his room until a strange woman came and led him to the bathroom where he stayed in the bathtub until the firemen came to save him. That's when the woman disappeared and, no, he did not know her.

"No matter how many times they talked to him, he stuck to that story," Sheila says. "I'm not sure if they thought he did something or not, but they talked to him many times until I finally put my foot down and told them no more."

As the weeks passed, it was finally determined that the cause of the fire appeared to be a space heater in the basement, where her son's body was found. The body of Danny's mother was found in her bedroom, his uncle's body was in the living room and his sister's body was found in her upstairs bedroom. But what happened in that house the night of the fire, no one knows for sure. Autopsies confirmed that the most likely cause of death for all the victims was smoke inhalation, but investigators refused to close the file because there were too many unanswered questions.

"They have never really come right out and accused my son of doing something that night that caused the fire, but I'm certain they blame him," Sheila says, admitting that she, too, wonders if he was somehow behind the fatal blaze.

"I don't like to think that he'd do something that would lead to the death of his wife and children, but I know we can't always understand how things work out. I know my son had a bad temper, but I'm not sure he was capable of something like that. But we will never know for certain."

As for Danny, he went to live at his grandparents' home and has been doing well despite the trauma he endured. But whenever he talks about that night, he continues to describe the mysterious woman as friendly and helpful. However, no one has been able to determine who she was.

"But," Sheila says, "I believe the woman was an angel sent to help Danny through all the bad stuff. Why him? I don't know, but I'm thankful that he made it and he's come to be with us."

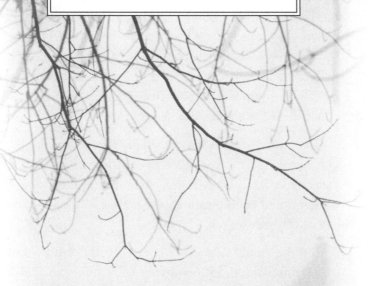

PART IV
The Message Within

In Her Dreams

LIKE THEIR COUNTERPARTS THE GHOSTS, angels appear out of nowhere and always without warning or notice, but unlike ghosts, they usually leave the person with a sense of calmness and even serenity. Ruby, a 43-year-old woman who lives in a quaint hamlet on Nova Scotia's South Shore, not far from the province's capital city, Halifax, says that's kind of how she felt when she had her experience.

"I know this sounds like something out of a science fiction movie, but I swear this happened to me," says Ruby, who now believes that even though life throws us curveballs, it also gives us many pleasures, and in the end, the good and bad usually balance out.

And she should know. Seven years ago, following a routine mammogram, doctors discovered a tumor in Ruby's left breast.

"Even though they had not yet determined if the tumor was cancerous or not, the news was devastating to me," she recalls, her voice cracking. "My grandmother died from breast cancer, and I watched a very close friend go through years of painful treatments because of breast cancer, only to die in the end. I thought this was the end of my world, and I guess in many ways it was, but today I've also become a different, stronger person, and I'm determined not to let this disease beat me."

Following a series of tests, doctors concluded that although the tumor was not yet malignant, she should have the lump removed and undergo a series of chemotherapy and radiation treatments to destroy any cancer cells that might be present. It would be an arduous schedule, but there was no other way to ensure she would recover.

"I knew what to expect," Ruby says, reflecting on the day they gave her the news. "It was going to be hard. I knew that. Thank God I had a good support system in place with my family and friends, but I knew what was coming. Even though I tried to remain strong, there were times when I just couldn't take it any more and I'd break down and cry, sometimes in the worst places like when I was in a restaurant or when I was driving. I even broke down once when I was visiting my kids' school. It was hard…very hard. Anyone who has ever gone through anything like this will understand just how difficult it is."

It was following one of those emotional breakdowns that Ruby discovered she has an angel watching over her.

"I was feeling especially exhausted this one particular day. It was only a few weeks before Christmas, and I had nothing done, not even a present bought," she says.

"I had just completed my third chemo treatment and I was very sick. Usually, it took me a day or so to get back on my feet following the treatment, and during this time, I felt really bad. I hurt all over. I was depressed and I was feeling sorry for myself. I just felt like I was at the end of my rope and didn't know where to turn."

Ruby's husband continued to work—"he had to"—but her family and friends always stayed with her for at least 24 hours following a treatment.

"My sister was like an angel, but she's not the angel I'm talking about. They were really worried about me because I was in a pretty bad state," she says. "I guess I gave them lots of reasons to be worried, but anyone who has gone through something like this will understand the place I was in.... It wasn't good."

Sleep was the only relief Ruby could find; it took her mind off her situation and allowed her to escape from the pain, so that's what she did.

"I slept a lot in those days. I just didn't feel like doing anything else," she says. On that particular day, she thinks she had been sleeping for maybe two hours when the vision came to her.

"I was asleep, yes," Ruby explains, "but what I saw that day was not like any dream I had ever had before or any I've had since then. Some people might say it was the drugs, but I don't think so."

As Ruby slept, a vision entered her subconscious, and she believes it was a messenger—an angel.

"It was so real. It was in my head, but it was like we were in the same place," she says. "I was sound asleep when I heard a voice. It was so calm and soothing. I finally felt relaxed and at peace. I hadn't felt that way for a long time, but suddenly this feeling of calmness just kind of washed over me. It was a strange sensation, and I knew from that point on I'd be okay."

In her vision, Ruby says an entity "that had a kind of glow around it," told her to keep the faith and to remain strong. "She said that while I was going through a tough time right then, I'd survive the ordeal and would be fine. She told me to keep fighting. I call it a woman, but I can't say for sure it was female. But I can tell you its voice was soft and soothing, sort of like the kind of voice a mother uses when she's snuggling her baby. That's what I think of when I recall the voice, and it was very comforting."

The vision lasted only a few minutes, and then Ruby suddenly woke up.

"From then on, I felt like a totally different person. I was more relaxed, and I actually saw my situation from a different perspective. For starters, instead of feeling sorry for myself and being depressed that they had discovered the tumor, I finally began to see how lucky I was that they had actually found it when they did, before it had a chance to turn into cancer. I just got up and felt so much better than I had in a very long time.... You just don't get that kind of feeling from a normal dream. This was more than that."

Although Ruby is convinced that an angel visited her while she was asleep, others around her remained skeptical about her vision, but they noted the change in her mental and emotional status. Her sister has embraced the idea and suggests that maybe it was their grandmother who spoke to her from the other side.

"I don't know about that…but maybe. I guess anything is possible," Ruby says.

However, not everyone is convinced that her "vision" was anything more than some sort of dream.

"My husband actually wondered if I was over-medicated, but I tell him that this had nothing to do with the medication. I really believe this vision was an angel sent to me to ease my suffering, and I really don't care what others think," she says. "I'd like for people to believe me, but I know what I saw and how it made me feel, and for me, that's all that matters."

Today, Ruby's cancer has not returned, and she continues to remain strong and healthy, determined to live a long life.

You Never Walk Alone

PEOPLE GET OLD AND PEOPLE DIE. These two realities are facts of life that no one can escape. Regardless of what we know, however, it is still never easy to let go of a loved one, even those who have become seriously ill and even when we sometimes know that death is inevitable, perhaps within hours.

For Holly Simmons of Halifax, letting go of her mother, Elizabeth, was the most heart-breaking thing she has ever had to do, but she eventually accepted that it meant the suffering would end for her mother.

When Elizabeth got sick and then had a stroke in 2002, Holly vowed that she would remain by her side and help her through the ordeal. Doctors told Holly that her mother would never recover, but she wanted to be with her every step of the way, no matter how difficult it would become. As she says, it's what children should do for their parents.

"It goes way beyond obligation," she says. "It's just something you must do. There was never any question that I'd be there for her."

Since Holly's father had died three years earlier, and her only sibling, a brother, lived in British Columbia, she was the only immediate family Elizabeth had. That meant that all the decisions about her mother's care and all her personal business fell on Holly's shoulders. As a mother of two teen-aged children and the wife of a hardworking career man, Holly found the responsibilities daunting and, at times, over-whelming, but she vowed she would never let her mother be alone. No matter how long Elizabeth had left on this earth, Holly promised her that she would be by her side, and for the first two years, she moved her mother in with her family.

"It wasn't always easy, I will admit that," Holly says, recalling those years during which she somehow man-aged to juggle her family life, taking care of her own home and caring for her invalid mother. Eventually, the burden became too much for her, so for everyone's sake, doctors recommended that Elizabeth be placed in a nursing home.

"I felt so guilty even entertaining the idea," Holly says, clearly still harboring some regret after all this time for hav-ing to even consider other options. "I know it was getting to where she was becoming too much for me to handle, and her doctor told me that for my own health and well-being, it would be best to put her in a facility where they are equipped to deal with people in her condition. They all told me it was for the best, and I guess maybe it was, but I had a hard time getting over the fact that it felt like I was letting her down.… In my mind, it was like I was abandoning her. I know I wasn't, but that's what it seemed like."

Holly came to realize that she would be of no use to her mother if she became so worn down that she herself also became sick, so she reluctantly admitted her mother to a nursing home. After Elizabeth entered the facility, Holly made a commitment to visit her mother every day. And for the two years that her mother was in the home, Holly never missed a day.

"Sometimes I could only have short visits with her, but I made an effort to drop in every day to see her," Holly says, adding that while the staff at the nursing home told her it wasn't necessary for her to come every day because it was unlikely her mother knew she was present, she went anyway. "I just couldn't abandon her. I felt I had to go, even when it wasn't clear that she knew I was there. I knew I wouldn't be able to live with myself if something happened to her and I hadn't seen her."

Besides, it didn't matter what the doctor told her, Holly was convinced that her mother knew she was there.

"They might have said that Mom didn't know what was happening around her, and they may have been right because they were trained to deal with people in that condition, but I believed otherwise," Holly says. "I had no medical proof to support my beliefs so I just called it a daughter's intuition, but I got the feeling that every time I walked into her room, Mom changed. She couldn't say anything and she couldn't move, but I'm convinced that she knew I was there."

Whenever Holly brought the subject up with the doctors and nurses, they told her it was normal for her to feel that way because people see what they want to see when a loved one is seriously ill.

"I think they were humoring me," she says. "They told me it was natural that I'd want to see these manifestations, but they also stressed that there was no way Mom could respond to my presence. In her condition, they said, she just wasn't capable of any communication, and it was doubtful that she was even aware of me.... I couldn't accept that. I just couldn't."

So, it was with that conviction and total commitment that Holly made the daily trip to the nursing home where some days she did nothing but just be there to keep her mother company.

"Some days I read to her and some days I turned on the television for company because Mom never talked.... She couldn't," Holly says.

"But that didn't matter. I'd talk to her and fill her in on the latest news around town and I'd tell her about what my kids were doing. She was always close to her grandchildren, and I believed my company made a difference to her so I kept coming and I kept talking to her. Maybe it was just to make myself feel better, I don't know, but I don't think so. I really thought that maybe hearing my voice would help keep Mom relaxed and in some ways might stimulate her mind.... Who really knows what I thought?"

During the many weeks and months that Holly spent sitting by her mother's bedside, she saw little improvement or few signs that Elizabeth heard her words. The massive stroke had left the woman totally paralyzed, incapable of even the smallest movement or communication.

"The stroke did a job on her, there was little doubt about that," Holly says with a deep sigh as tears well in her eyes. "In fact, the stroke was so severe that they said she was lucky to still be alive...if you can say that being confined to your bed 24 hours a day, seven days a week without so much as even a single word as being lucky, well, then, I guess you could say she was lucky. To me, it was the ultimate life sentence, and seeing her like that was really hard on me."

And, she adds, "I guess that's what was so difficult for me to understand. Why had this happened to her? She'd been such a good person. She had been a great mother and a wonderful homemaker. In my opinion, she didn't deserve any of what happened to her. It just seemed so undignified to have to live the last few years of her life in that condition. She'd always been the kind of woman who took such care of her personal appearance, so to see her like that was really sad.… I know she wouldn't have wanted to live like that, but what choice do you have? Keeping her comfortable was the only option."

That is why, after witnessing her mother's physical condition deteriorate for several years, Holly was totally amazed "beyond belief" when, during one of her visits, Elizabeth began talking to her.

"I swear to God it happened," Holly says with such conviction that it is impossible not to believe her. "It totally caught me off guard, and most people don't believe it happened. The doctors, my husband and even my brother tell me it was just my emotions taking over, that and the fact that I was totally exhausted. But I know it happened…I know it, and no one will ever convince me otherwise."

It was a Tuesday evening and Holly was visiting the nursing home as she did every weekday after supper. She figures she had been with her mother for about 15 or 20 minutes "and I was chatting away like I always did, telling her about the kids and stuff like that when suddenly, out of the blue, she says to me, 'Who's that man over there?'"

Holly pauses, as if collecting her thoughts, then continues.

After calming herself down and ringing for the nurse, Holly asked, "What man, Mom? What man over where?"

Holly insists that no one else was in the room with them. Usually, whenever she visited, it was just the two of them, so if there had been anyone else around, she most certainly would have noticed.

"What man, Mom?" she asked again, hoping that the nurse would hurry up and get there.

"Who's that man over there?" Elizabeth asked again.

Despite what others tried to tell her, Holly remains convinced that she heard her mother speak those words not once, but twice.

"No one believes me," she says. By the time the nurse got to the room, her mother had once again become comatose, not responding to any stimulus whatsoever. "When I told the nurse that Mom had spoke and what she had said, she looked at me like I had two heads or something like that. I know she thought I was nuts, but I also know what I heard. I'd like for others to believe me, but just because they don't believe it, doesn't mean it didn't happen."

Thinking back on it in the days that followed the incident, Holly is not only convinced that her mother spoke to her, but she also now believes that the man whom Elizabeth saw in the room that evening was, in fact, an angel.

"It wasn't my emotions, and, yes, I was tired, but I wasn't that tired that I imagined my mother speaking," Holly says. "She said those words just as clear as anything I can say right now. And if there was a man in that room, then it had to be an angel."

And, considering that her mother's health took a turn for the worse by the end of the week, and that by the week-end, she had died, Holly says she is even more convinced an angel was there watching over her mother as the end was drawing near.

"I didn't want to lose her, but I also didn't want her suffering to continue," Holly says. "Mom had gone through so much and had suffered in so many ways that her death was really a godsend. When they phoned me at home that Friday night and told me I should come right over to the nursing home, I wasn't all that surprised."

A few hours later, with Holly and other family members beside her, Elizabeth slowly drifted away.

"Was it hard? Yes, without question, it was one of the hardest experiences I have ever had in my entire life," she says, fighting to keep her emotions under control. "To stand there and watch your mother die is not easy, but I also had this feeling in my heart that she wasn't going alone. As Mom left us, I just kept thinking of something she used to say—you never walk alone."

In this case, Holly believes that her mother wasn't alone.

"It all made sense to me," she says. "Not only that Mom had spoken to me after all those years of not being able to talk, but the fact that she was obviously seeing a man in her room was just too much of a coincidence for me. I really think Mom knew her end was near and that she had accepted it. Once she did, an angel came to make her last days on earth more comfortable because, when I think about what had happened, I remember that she had changed after that day. It's like there was a new sense of calmness around her."

Before this incident, Holly never really thought herself to be a particularly spiritual person, but she admits something has changed in the way she now approaches the topic.

"I don't think you have to be a die-hard religious person to believe in miracles," she says, adding that her mother's illness and subsequent death taught her that faith could mean different things to different people. "Religious people don't have a corner on the faith market. I believe that if you live a clean, wholesome life and you treat other people with respect and dignity, then you have every reason to expect that in the end, you will receive your ultimate reward. I believe that's what happened in Mom's case."

Does Holly believe there is a heaven?

"I don't know. I like to think so, and if there is, I believe that's where Mom has gone," she says. "But I certainly believe an angel was with her at the end, and in many ways, that makes me feel better."

All in Her Head

THINKING BACK ON HOW QUICKLY the accident happened, Rosemary Hampton can't recall seeing the car barreling down on her, nor can she remember the moment it struck her body, but she knows that the event changed how she views her existence. Besides landing her in the hospital for nearly two months and giving her a series of recurring aches and pains that will affect her mobility probably until the day she dies, the accident left her with a new appreciation for the unexplained mysteries of life.

Five years ago, Rosemary was an average, middle-aged woman living in Minneapolis, Minnesota. She had a great job as a sales clerk at a clothing outlet, was dating a wonderful man with whom she was planning to spend the rest her life, had a long list of good friends and enjoyed the company of her three pet beagles, Penny, Rocky and Zeus. But her entire life changed in an instant on that day in April. While out for a late afternoon run along her favorite route that took her through some of the city's tree-lined streets, for whatever reason she can't remember, Rosemary didn't see the car as it swerved and struck her from behind. The last thing she remembers is flying through the air and striking the pavement. After that, everything went black.

According to what she's been told about the accident, the driver of the car, an elderly man, said he swerved to avoid hitting a cat and didn't see the runner in front of him. By the time he noticed the young woman, it was too late to avoid her. Before he could react, his car slammed into her and sent her flying several yards ahead of his vehicle. She smashed into the pavement with such force that dozens of bones in her body were shattered upon impact. Within 15 minutes, rescue personnel had arrived and Rosemary was in an ambulance on her way to the hospital. Doctors worked on her for several hours, repairing broken bones in her legs and arms, stitching up cuts and basically keeping her alive. But she doesn't remember any of it.

"Nothing," she says. "Not a thing. The entire ordeal is a total blackout to me. All I know about what happened that day is what people have told me, but I guess I gave everyone a pretty good scare. Indeed she did. In fact, doctors told Rosemary's fiancé and her parents that considering the extent of her injuries, there was a good chance she would never walk again, as both of her legs were shattered from the force of the impact.

But more alarming was that she was in a coma from the severe blow she had taken to her head. Based upon their examination, doctors said there didn't appear to be any serious brain trauma, but because she was unconscious, they couldn't determine what long-term damage, if any, she may have suffered. Tests to determine the full extent of those injuries could only be carried out once she came around. Until then, all they could do was keep her comfortable and control the pain. Her fate, they said, was in someone else's hands.

"Imagine what that would be like," Rosemary says. "I had no idea what was happening to me. I was totally vulnerable, yet I knew nothing about this. As far as I was concerned, I was gone. My body may have been still alive, but I was locked away in my own mind and was oblivious to the world around me."

Rosemary believes it's a good thing that she doesn't remember any of those days because she isn't sure how she would have handled the news that she may not walk again, let alone the physical pain.

"I consider myself to be a pretty free-spirited person. I'm used to coming and going as I please. I don't like to depend on anyone," she says. "If I'd been awake and the doctors had told me they weren't sure that I'd be able to walk again, I wouldn't have been able to handle it. I can't imagine what it would be like to be told something like that. How do you cope?"

As it was, she didn't have to deal with that news right away, and on one level, Rosemary says, that's a good thing.

"I won't lie to you and say I would've been brave and strong and all those things we're supposed to be in the face of adversity," she says. "I'd have lost it. I'm pretty sure of that."

However, Rosemary believes being in a coma was actually someone's way of protecting her from all of the stress and pain that would have come with having to deal with the grim prognosis.

"I'm not saying it was a good thing or that I was lucky to be in a coma," she says. "That would be crazy. But I do believe our bodies and minds take steps to protect us from certain trauma. It's possible that my mind slipped into a coma as a way of helping me face this ordeal and to shield me from the pain."

Whatever the reason, Rosemary was in a coma for almost five days following the accident, during which, she says, she had no idea of what was happening around her.

"I don't remember anything from the time I hit the pavement to the day I woke up in the hospital bed with all those tubes and wires running from my body," she says. "Or let me say I don't remember anything that was happening in the real world during that time."

In truth, she does have memories of that time, but they're not memories of the accident, the hospital or her friends and family worrying over her. Instead, she has memories of visions that she can't explain. She believes they began almost immediately after the accident. While it's difficult for Rosemary to explain how she felt during this time, the experience was unlike anything she had ever had before.

"When I say everything went black, what I mean is that everything went black in this world," she says. "But in the world in my head, there was bright lights and lots of vivid colors. It was a cheery and happy place, and I felt light as a feather. It was kind of like I was floating all the time."

While locked in her own mind, Rosemary had no concept of time or space, nor was she aware of the pain that apparently, based on her injuries, she should have been suffering.

"But I wasn't aware of any of that," she says. "It's like, while I was locked in this space in my mind, nothing could hurt me."

On the downside, while Rosemary was in this coma, she couldn't communicate with anyone, and that's what bothered her the most.

"I understand that my family and friends were worrying about me, and if I could have, I would've told them that they could stop fretting because I was okay. But I couldn't speak. I couldn't even move, so there was no way of letting them know," she says.

Although she had no awareness of the outside world, eventually, in her own world, she met a man dressed in white who reached out to her, and she immediately felt warm and relaxed.

"I'm not exactly sure when I met him, but I remember thinking how peaceful this man made me feel and how he seemed to embrace me with his warmth," she says. "I have no idea who he was or if he had a name, but I know that I felt safe with him."

The man didn't speak, but he remained with her during the duration of her ordeal until finally, he spoke, and when he did, his voice was soothing and gentle.

"He just told me, 'It's not time yet,'" she says. "That's it. I don't remember him ever saying anything else."

And with that, Rosemary woke from her coma to find herself lying in a hospital bed with her fiancé and parents gathered around her.

"It was a total shock," she recalls. "One second I was in this warm, friendly place where there is no pain, with this man who made me feel so safe and secure, then the next thing I know, I'm in a hospital room with all this fuss and confusion. I had no idea what was happening to me because I didn't remember the accident or anything that had happened over the past five days."

Immediately, doctors began poking and prodding Rosemary in an effort to determine the extent of her injuries.

"I remember thinking how badly I wanted to disappear to that world inside my head again where everything was so peaceful and calm," she says.

It was all overwhelming at first, but in time, Rosemary had to come to grips with the reality of her situation. She required several operations to repair the broken bones in her legs, and she underwent months of physiotherapy, but eventually she regained her strength and was able to return to her normal routine.

"But it certainly wasn't easy. I'll admit that. It was a tough struggle, but I got through it with the support of my family and friends. They were all so wonderful," she says.

Even after all these years since the accident, Rosemary still has no recollection of those five days she lost while she was in the coma.

"Not a second of it," she says. "I can't remember a thing. When something does come back, it's all fuzzy and hazy, as if I'm looking through a window covered in condensation."

Honestly, though, she doesn't want to remember those days.

"Why would I? I imagine I was in so much pain that it was unbearable, and I'm convinced that's why my mind was kept in a coma," she says. "It was so I wouldn't have to face all of that. I believe it was my body's way of helping me heal."

Instead of memories of those dark days, Rosemary has memories of that world in her head.

"I choose to hang on to those. I have no idea what that place was, or who that man was, but I honestly believe he was an angel sent to be with me and to make me feel comfortable. If that's what heaven is like, then I guess that's where I was.

Straight to the Heart

WHEN THE DOCTOR TOLD TOM JOHNSTON that he needed to have heart bypass surgery before his condition worsened, the first thought that ran through his mind was that he had to make sure his closet was cleaned out before going to the hospital.

"I know it sounds strange," says the 57-year-old former forester, who always considered himself to be healthy. But he wasn't thinking about himself at that moment.

To begin with, Tom found it difficult to believe that he had a heart problem, let alone that he would require surgery to fix it. He did not smoke or consume alcohol except for a few occasional social drinks, and he had never had a sick day in his life until he had a minor heart attack shortly after his birthday two years earlier. But once he heard the diagnosis, the only thing he could think about was how difficult it would be for his wife, Carrie, to have to clean out his closet and get rid of all his belongings should something go wrong during the surgery and he didn't make it.

"I think when you're facing something like that, your mind reacts in strange ways," Tom says. "And I bet everyone reacts differently."

Although Tom understood that because of advances in medicine and technology the procedure he required was now pretty much considered routine, he knew risks were still involved. The doctors would remove a vein from his thigh and use it to construct a bypass around his heart and, unless complications arose, he would be in hospital three or four days at the most.

"They told me not worry," he recalls. "They said it was pretty routine and that considering the physical shape I was in, everything should go well with the surgery. They said they do this all the time and have a good success rate."

However, despite the assurances from the heart specialist and his own family doctor—a man he had known for over 20 years—Tom also realized there were always risks with any surgery.

"It doesn't matter how minor the surgery is, I understand there's always a chance something could go wrong," he says, instinctively rubbing his chest as if to reassure himself that he had survived the procedure. "And no matter what they say, the doctors don't really know for sure what kind of complications they may run into once they start the surgery, so I know nothing like this is ever 100 percent guaranteed."

They were, after all, going to cut open his chest.

"I'd be lying if I said I wasn't nervous about the surgery. I don't care how big and brave you think you are, to me, the prospect of going under the knife and having someone mess around with my heart didn't sit too well with me, but they told me it had be done if I want to live, so what choice did I have?"

Besides, the odds really were in his favor.

"They do several of these procedures every day, so they know what they're doing," he says, "and, as my doctor told me, I was in otherwise good health, so while he couldn't guarantee me that there would be no problems, he reassured me that he expected I would have a quick and full recovery."

But, like everything else, Tom says there's always a chance that something might not go as planned.

"That's what bothered me," he says, quickly adding, "I guess maybe that's why I thought about how Carrie would cope with doing something as simple as cleaning out my closet if I didn't pull through. Thankfully, it never came to that, but I did have issues."

Tom's surgery was scheduled for a Monday morning and, after giving his family the usual hugs and kisses, he was wheeled into the operating room and put under. Up until then, everything seemed to be running like clockwork.

"It all seemed to be pretty smooth to me," he recalls. "The doctors and nurses were relaxed, and I found that reassuring because it allowed me to calm down."

But it was after he was asleep that he had an unusual experience that will remain with him for the rest of his life, and it certainly changed his perspective. The doctors told him afterwards that the anesthetic had caused him to hallucinate, but he believes it was more than that.

"I saw an angel when I was stretched out on that operating table," Tom states without hesitation, explaining that his vision was too vivid and detailed for it not to have been something more than a dream.

"No way," he insists. "I just can't believe it was all in my head, like they tell me it was."

Describing his vision, Tom admits he lost track of time once they gave him a sedative to help him relax, so he has no idea how long he was under before he became aware of his surroundings.

"Now, don't misunderstand me," he explains. "I'm not saying that I woke up during the surgery, because I didn't. I was out of it. I couldn't move and I couldn't feel a thing, but somehow I could see the operating room, and I could see the doctors and nurses moving around…. It's like I was kind of outside my body, yet still inside my body. It's hard to describe, and the doctors tell me there's no way I would've been aware of anything that was going on in there. They said it's normal for surgical patients to hallucinate when they're starting to come out of the anesthetic, but I wasn't imagining anything. I know I wasn't."

Explaining his vision, Tom says he experienced the most calming sensation he has ever felt. It was like a wave of tranquility washed over him.

"I was totally relaxed," he says. "I remember it felt like I didn't have a worry in the world, despite the fact that I was undergoing major surgery right at that moment. I probably should have been scared, but I was so calm. I can't describe how good I felt. I don't think any drug could ever make you feel that good."

In that relaxed state of mind, Tom insists that he saw a white image moving around the operating room, although he could not distinguish its exact characteristics.

"I can't tell you if it was a man or a woman…it was more or less kind of like an outline of someone, and it was sort of flimsy that I could see through it, but it was there and it was moving around the room between the doctors and nurses."

Tom vividly recalls seeing it pause beside the surgeon who was performing the procedure, and it remained there for several seconds.

"I know this is weird," he continues, "but it was almost like this thing—whatever it was—was inspecting the surgeon's work. Strange as I know that sounds, I remember thinking that's exactly what it seemed like to me."

Hours later, after the surgery was done and Tom was in the recovery room starting to emerge from the anesthetic, he somehow knew he would be okay. But he could also tell that something wasn't quite right.

"I think it may have been the look of worry on Carrie's face that greeted me when I woke up, but I knew right away that something had gone wrong during the surgery," he says. Tom learned that his blood pressure had dropped to such dangerously low levels during his surgery that the doctors were concerned he might suffer another heart attack right there on the table. Occasionally, the doctors told him, they do encounter those types of complications, but they were able to intervene and he should be okay. However, the blood pressure issue meant that he had been in surgery longer than had been anticipated.

Upon hearing the news, Tom didn't know how to react. Inexplicably, his first reaction was one of relief.

"I know it sounds nuts," he admits, "but I wasn't panicked or worried or even concerned that I could have died in there. I don't think that's a normal reaction to that kind of news, but I just knew everything was okay and I was going to be fine."

At first, Tom decided not to tell anyone about his experience in the operating room because, honestly, he felt that no one would believe him.

"And why would they?" he states. "I know it sounds far-fetched, but I know what I saw." But in the end, he couldn't keep the secret bottled up any longer. The first person he told was Carrie.

"She just looked at me like I was an alien or something," he recalls with a shrug. "And why wouldn't she?"

Angels in the operating room?

Tom agrees it did sound too extraordinary to believe, but eventually Carrie accepted that he did have some sort of life-altering experience during his surgery.

"She doesn't press me on it," he says, adding, however, that the doctors dismiss his vision as the effects from the anesthetic.

"But they have a scientific mind so maybe they aren't able to let themselves believe that these things can happen," Tom reasons. "But the fact is, I'm sure they happen all the time. Just because someone doesn't believe they can happen doesn't mean it's not real.... It certainly felt real to me. All I can tell you is what I know, and I know what I saw. People can decide for themselves if they believe it or not.... I can't control what people think, but I can tell you it changed my life."

Perhaps it was his encounter with the unknown, but following his ordeal, Tom became more aware of the little things in life that most people take for granted. He considers his second chance to be a gift, and he intends to make the most of it.

And, for the record, before going to the hospital for his surgery, he did clean out his closet.

A Mother's Best Friend

WE ALL HAVE DAYS DURING WHICH we wish we would have just stayed in bed with the covers pulled over our heads, but the reality in life is that most of us simply cannot do that. Those of us with a family, a job and other responsibilities must force ourselves to get up and go about our business, no matter how bad we feel. And usually, once we get up and begin doing our jobs, carrying out our routines and mingling with others, most of our troubles seem to go away…but not always.

Everything in Tina Weston's life was going according to plan. She was a mother of two young, active children. She had a successful consulting business that she ran from her home so she could be there when her seven-year-old son, Alex, and his older sister, Julia, returned from school. Tina's husband is a high school teacher, and the couple has a wonderful, modern home. She thought she had the perfect life until one day, a few years back, when it seemed as though her world was about to crash down around her.

The day started off badly, she recalls, noting that she has always had a special extra sense about such things.

"It's uncanny, really," she admits with a hint of trepidation. However, after collecting her thoughts, she continues, "Sometimes I just seem to know when something is going to happen, but most times I just shrug it off. It's just this strange feeling I get…. I can't explain it. Maybe it's intuition, but I do seem to be tuned in to the world around me more than most people. Now, I'm not saying I'm psychic or anything extraordinary like that, but sometimes I do get these feelings, and when I get them, it often does…it freaks me out sometimes."

Tina gets up every morning at six o'clock. She likes to have a coffee, check the news and get herself organized before calling the children and getting them off to school.

"I don't know why, but that particular morning when the alarm went off, something just felt wrong," Tina says, recalling the events of that late September day. "Everything was kind of off kilter. I just knew it was going to be a bad day. I think everyone has those days, and I really hate them. They throw me for a loop, and I usually don't function well."

But on this morning, she knew her mood was more than the normal doldrums.

"It was a pretty strong feeling that something was really wrong," she says, adding that she wished she could just stay in bed because maybe she could avoid whatever was going to happen.

But Tina knew she couldn't. She had commitments. "I haven't been able to stay in bed all day since I was 13," she says with a chuckle. It is a welcome injection of humor, and her face immediately lights up when she smiles, but her mood quickly turns serious once again.

After going through her normal morning routine, Tina set about doing her work. She structures her day so that she can have her work completed by the time the children return home from school around three so she can spend time with them before starting dinner. It's all very organized.

"But that's my life. I know I'm anal, but I have to have a schedule if I'm going to function and get anything done.... But no matter how hard I worked that day, I couldn't shake the feeling that something wasn't right," she says, pausing, then pushing onward as she recalls the events as they unfolded. "I tried to keep busy, but something just kept nagging at me. I just couldn't shake the feeling that something bad was going to happen, and I hated how it made me feel."

By the time Alex and Julia got home from school that afternoon, Tina was ready to call it a day.

"I hadn't been very productive anyway," she admits. "Although I did have a report due by the end of the week, I hadn't made much progress on it, so I thought maybe if I got away from it overnight and came back to it the next morning with a fresh set of eyes, then I might get somewhere."

What she didn't know, however, was that when she shut down her office that afternoon, it would be several more weeks before she would return to her work. When the children came home, Alex asked, because it was a warm day, if he could go outside and ride bikes with a couple of his friends. Tina said he could go, but she also insisted that he wear his helmet.

"I know some kids don't always use helmets when they ride bikes or go skateboarding, but we've always made Alex and Julia wear them," she says. "Even when they were just learning how to ride their tricycles, we made them wear helmets. That way, we figured, they'd get used to wearing them, and Julia is always good about using hers but sometimes Alex needs reminding. He'll wear it, reluctantly, because he knows if he doesn't, he will not be allowed to ride his bike, but he doesn't like it much, especially when some of the other kids never wear one."

However, Alex knows the rules—no helmet, no bike.

"That's simply the way it is in our household," Tina asserts. "That is never open to debate."

Today, Alex has a better appreciation of his parents' position on bike helmets because he knows wearing a helmet that afternoon most likely saved his life—that, and he had an angel watching over him.

Tina estimates the kids were outside for about half an hour when Julia came running into the kitchen where Tina was busily preparing dinner. Her daughter was in tears and was really worked up.

"She was in a real bad way," Tina recalls, then pauses, as if collecting her thoughts. "Then she just blurted out that Alex had fallen off his bike and was hurt."

Tina panicked because, as a parent, she immediately thought the worst. Alex was a carefree kid who often pushed the limit, throwing caution to the wind, and it was possible that Julia was overacting.

"But I didn't think so," Tina continues. "Julia was used to Alex's stunts, and she had seen him take spills many times before. If she was upset, then I knew it must be pretty bad… and it was."

Rushing out the door and following her daughter down the road, Tina could see her son sprawled in a ditch on a pile of rocks, and he didn't appear to be moving. As she got closer, she saw that he was bleeding from around his nose and mouth, which suggested possible internal injuries to her. She was frantic. Alex didn't respond when she called out his name, and he was not moving.

"I knew it wasn't good," she recalls, wiping tears from her eyes as she relives the emotions she felt that day. "I also knew I shouldn't move him because there could be some spinal injuries, and moving him might make them worse."

Tina always carried her work cell phone with her, even at home, so she quickly called 911 as well as her husband, who had not yet come home from work because of a school basketball game. Within minutes, the ambulance and her husband arrived at the scene.

"I was freaking out," Tina says, explaining that the other kids told her Alex had dared them that he could make the jump across the ditch, but that he had to be going really fast in order to do so. To achieve that speed, he went to the top of a hill and barreled down the slope at break-neck speed. When he neared the ditch, his bike's front tire skidded on some loose gravel, causing him to lose control of the bike. The bike flipped over, and Alex landed on his back. He didn't get up, the other kids told her.

"I didn't know the extent of his injuries, but I could tell he was banged up pretty bad," Tina says. It was difficult for her to stand by and let the paramedics do their job. As a mother, she wanted to be right in there to help her child.

"But my husband held me back," she says. "He kept me out of the way so they could work, but that was hard for me."

Following an initial examination of Alex at the scene, the paramedics slowly moved him—helmet and all—to a stretcher and then to the ambulance. He was immediately transferred to the hospital. Tina and her husband followed behind while Julia stayed with a neighbor.

It was several more hours before the Westons finally heard the news...and it wasn't good.

"They told us that Alex had some internal bleeding but that wasn't their biggest worry," she explains, wiping away tears again. "Their first concern was that he had suffered some serious head injuries. While the helmet had cushioned the blow, they were still concerned that there was major swelling around the brain. They also told us that he would have to be transferred to the Halifax [children's] hospital, and I freaked out. I just lost it right there in the corridor. It was a nightmare come true for me...it would be for any parent."

Because doctors were worried the swelling might worsen, they told the Westons they were going to keep Alex sedated and wanted to transport him as quickly as possible. How could her day turn into this, Tina wondered. "I just knew something was going to happen, but I never dreamed it would be something that would affect one of my children like this."

Later that evening, Alex was transported, via ambulance, to the regional children's hospital in Halifax, two hours away from their home, where he would receive specialized care. Tina went with him in the ambulance while her husband followed in their car.

"It was my worst fear coming true," she recalls. "We had no idea how serious Alex's injuries were or if he would recover, and if he did recover, we didn't know if there would be long-term effects. I was beside myself, and I prayed the whole way to Halifax."

Upon arrival at the hospital, Alex underwent a battery of tests, and after many hours, the doctors finally gave his parents some results.

"The waiting was the hardest part," she says. "Not knowing what was going on with Alex was nerve-wracking, that's for sure. It's hard to remain calm when one of your children is in that shape and you have no idea what's going on. You just want to be with them and hold them and make everything all right for them."

The doctors determined that Alex's brain had been bruised when his head smacked the rocks, and there was no way of telling how long he would be unconscious or if he would have any serious long-term effects. The doctors warned that there could be permanent brain damage, but all they could do was wait for him to wake up. He also broke his right arm and several ribs in the fall, which accounted for the internal bleeding. Those bones would mend, though.

"They also told us that it was a good thing Alex had been wearing his helmet because if he hadn't, then there was a good chance the impact would have killed him," Tina says. "That's pretty hard for a parent to hear, but I was thankful we had established the rules about helmets with our children, and I shuddered to think about what could have otherwise been that day."

As Alex's hospital stay stretched into days, Tina and her husband took shifts staying with their son.

"We never let him be alone," she explains. "One of us was always with him, but I always pulled down the night shift."

On the second night, Tina encountered a strange visitor to Alex's room. It was about three in the morning, and most of the hospital was in darkness except for some strategically placed nightlights.

"It was pretty dreary and quiet," Tina recalls. "And I was sleeping in the second bed in his room when I suddenly woke up because I could sense someone in the room with us. You know how you just feel it when someone's around? That's how it felt, and when I woke up, I was surprised to see a woman wearing a long, light-colored coat of some kind standing at the foot of Alex's bed. She was looking at him, almost admiring him. At first I thought it was a nurse, but I had gotten to know most of Alex's nurses and I didn't recognize her."

But then, as she talked with the strange woman, Tina realized that she didn't recognize the visitor, though this didn't seem to bother Tina.

"Maybe I should have been freaked out or concerned that some strange woman was hanging around Alex's bed, but I wasn't," she says. In truth, she suddenly felt calm, perhaps more calm than she had felt in the past few days.

"I just all of sudden felt very relaxed and comfortable with this woman, whoever she was," Tina says, recalling the conversation that followed.

"Can I help you?" Tina asked the woman.

"I'm here to check on Alex," the woman answered, and her voice was soft and very soothing. "He appears to be resting comfortably."

"Yes, he is," Tina said. "They have him heavily medicated. They say it's best that way."

"I'm sure it is," the woman continued.

"Who are you?" Tina finally asked. "Are you a nurse?"

"I'm just a friend," the woman said.

"A friend?" Tina replied. "Why have you come so late? Should you be here at this hour?"

"It doesn't matter," the woman replied. "I have a message for you."

"For me? What kind of message?" Tina pushed on, her curiosity piqued.

"I want to tell you that your son will be fine," the woman said.

"How can you know that?" Tina asked.

"Alex will make a full recovery," the woman continued.

"I appreciate that," Tina said. "But I'd like to know how you came to be here."

"I'm here," the woman said. "That's all that matters. I'm your friend, and I must tell you that everything will be okay."

With that, the woman disappeared.

"It was strange. It was like I blinked or something and the woman vanished," Tina recalls, but adds, "I wasn't alarmed or anything. In fact, it was just the opposite. I felt totally relaxed and relieved."

But she was curious about the woman.

Making her way to the nurses' desk, Tina asked about the woman who had just been in Alex's room and who must have surely passed by the station to get there.

"Both nurses who were on duty just looked at me like I was crazy," she says. "They insisted that they were both at the desk the whole while, and if anyone had gone in or out of Alex's room, they surely would have seen her. They were very insistent that no one was there.... But there was. I know there was. I had a conversation with someone that night, and I'm certain I didn't dream it."

Despite not knowing the identity of the visitor, Tina quickly fell back to sleep after she returned to the extra bed in Alex's room. And she slept very well, so well that she didn't even hear the nurses on their early rounds until one of them woke her up.

"She woke me to tell me that Alex was awake and that he seemed to be doing better. He was asking for me, the nurse said," Tina says, again wiping away the tears from her eyes. "I was overwhelmed with emotions and quickly called his father, who was already on his way to the hospital. I couldn't believe it, but I was so relieved. It was like someone had just removed a huge weight from my shoulders."

Indeed, Alex was sitting up in bed and sipping a glass of ice water, and he wanted to know what kind of shape his bike was in.

"I cried and laughed both at the same time," Tina says. "It was such an emotional experience to see my child functioning as if nothing had happened...."

Following several days of testing, doctors determined that Alex would fully recover, and they didn't anticipate any lasting effects from the accident.

"He was lucky. It really was a miracle," Tina says, explaining that once she had a chance to think about what the strange woman said that night, she determined that the visitor had been an angel.

"What else could it have been? The nurses didn't see her, and she knew so much about Alex's condition, so I'm convinced it was an angel. We experienced a miracle that night...I'm certain of that."

Now, two years later, Alex has fully recovered from the accident.

"To see him going on that bike today, you would never know that he had a near brush with death. He's so carefree," she says of her young son, "but now he doesn't argue when we tell him to put on his helmet."

Come to think of it, she adds with a smile, they hardly ever have to remind him.

Fighting Mad

MULTIPLE SCLEROSIS, OR MS, IS AN autoimmune disease that affects the central nervous system, which is the brain and spinal cord. MS usually occurs in women more than men, and the disorder most commonly begins between the ages of 20 and 40 but can strike at any age. The exact cause of MS is not known, but it is believed to result from damage to the myelin sheath, the protective material that surrounds nerve cells. It's a progressive disease, which means the nerve damage gets worse over time.

In addition to nerve damage, another part of MS is inflammation that occurs when the body's own immune cells attack the nervous system. The inflammation destroys the myelin, leaving multiple areas of scar tissue (sclerosis). It also causes nerve impulses to slow down or become blocked, leading to the symptoms of MS. Repeated episodes, or flare ups, of inflammation can appear along any area of the brain and spinal cord.

There is no cure for MS, and for people living with the disease, the idea of a possible cure offers different levels of hope to them. For those who have just been diagnosed, a cure might stop MS in its tracks. For Robin Ferguson, who has lived with MS for many years and has experienced loss of mobility and other serious impairments, a cure might repair the nervous system and allow her to recover lost functions. However, while major strides have been made in recent decades through research, a cure for MS continues to elude researchers. But sufferers remain hopeful that in time, the disease will be eradicated and no one will have to suffer the pain and indignities that Robin, and thousands of others, has endured in the years since being diagnosed when she was 24. She is now 29.

Robin had everything going for her. She had a great job that she loved. She worked as a paralegal in a Halifax-based law firm when she began feeling the first tremors in the little toe on her right foot. At first, she admits, she ignored the twitches, thinking they would eventually go away. But they didn't. In fact, not only did the twitches continue, they got worse. Eventually, she began experiencing other symptoms, including the occasional bouts of blurred vision, numbness in her fingers and toes and regular headaches.

"At first," she says, "I dismissed all of these symptoms as just being overstressed and tired because, while I loved my job, it was demanding, and I told myself that I probably wasn't getting enough sleep or taking good care of myself, so I just assumed that it was work related."

However, when she began to lose her balance and started stumbling about, she realized that there was something more to it than just being tired or stressed.

"Sometimes," Robin recalls, "I'd trip for no reason, and I'd shrug it off by saying I tripped over my own feet and I'd tell everyone that I was just clumsy."

But unbeknownst to Robin, these small occurrences were all symptoms of a much bigger problem.

After several months of putting off seeing her doctor, Robin finally gave in, and so began a whirlwind series of visits to various doctors and specialists, which in turn led to a seemingly unending battery of tests, including CT scans and MRIs that ultimately delivered the diagnosis—she had multiple sclerosis.

"I was devastated," the young woman admits, brushing tears from her eyes. Being unable to control her emotions is also one of the symptoms of MS, and she says in recent years that problem has gotten worse, along with slurred speech.

"However, even though I cry a lot, I've promised myself that I won't let this disease beat me," Robin says with a ferocity that conveys her resolve to fight this infliction that is slowly stealing her life. "I'm fighting mad that this is happening to me, but I gave up asking those questions a long time ago. It does no good to ask why I have this disease, because I know there are no answers. Why? Why? Why?… Why does someone get cancer? Why does someone have a heart attack or die in a car accident? You can't find any answers for these questions, so you just have to accept it and try to make the most of it."

But, she quickly adds, "That doesn't mean you have to give up, either. When you're given this kind of news, I figure you have two choices—either you roll over and die or you fight like hell to live and to be as healthy as you can. I went with the second choice."

However, Robin didn't always feel that way.

"When the doctors told me that they had finally found out what was wrong with me, I was devastated. I cried a lot, and I became angry and questioned why this was happening to me. I withdrew from all my family and friends, and they were all really worried about me," Robin explains. They had good reason to worry, because she was on the verge of self-destruction.

"There was a time when I thought about giving up and ending my life, I admit that, but then something happened that convinced me that I still had a lot to live for. Something happened that changed my life. I still have my bad days, naturally, but for the most part, I've accepted this is my life, and I've got no choice but to make myself keep going because I know that the minute I give up, this thing wins, and I won't let it beat me…. I refuse to let this get the best of me. I just won't."

It was shortly after her diagnosis when Robin was feeling especially bad about her predicament and struggling to come to terms with what was happening to her body that she had a revelation. She found it difficult to be around other people and preferred to have her privacy.

"I know my family and friends were concerned about me and they were all worried about how I was going to cope with this disease that was taking over my life, because at first I was a mess. I admit that. I wasn't very nice to those people who just wanted to help me through this, but it was impossible for me to feel anything except to feel sorry for myself. Honestly, I think most people go through these phases when life throws these curves at us, but eventually, I just said enough is enough, I can't live like this."

Robin says she had this epiphany one evening after she made her best friend, Jodie, leave her alone.

"I wasn't trying to be mean to Jodie, honestly," she recalls, "but I was having a really crappy day and going on about how I was going to have to quit my job, and I feared that my boyfriend was going to leave me and this and that to where I just told her to leave.... She had been a really good friend to me and had seen me through a lot. I should have been more kind to her, but I had reached my breaking point. I was freaking out, and I didn't want anyone around me. I just wanted to be alone, so I told Jodie she should go home. I know I was really rude, but Jodie was really good and she said she understood, but she didn't deserve to be treated like that. I was just so mean."

However, realizing that her friend was having a bad day, Jodie didn't argue. Instead, she made Robin promise to phone her in the morning, and then she left the apartment.

"After Jodie left, I took my medicines and went straight to bed," Robin recalls. Two or three hours later, she suddenly awoke with the feeling that someone else was in the bedroom with her. Even though Robin lived alone, some friends, including Jodie, have a key to the apartment so she automatically assumed that someone had come to check on her. "I knew people were worried about me so I thought that maybe Jodie had come back just to make sure I was okay."

"Jodie," Robin called out. "Is that you?"

There was no answer, so she called out again.

"Jodie? Did you come back?... Is there someone there?"

Still, there was no answer.

Finally, after lying in her bed for several minutes, Robin decided she should get up to investigate. Getting out of bed was a task for her. By this time, the disease had progressed to where she required a cane to help keep her balance, but she was able to slowly pull herself up and put her feet on the floor. Switching on the lamp on the table beside her bed, Robin fully expected to find someone in the room with her, but when the light came on, she was alone.

"I can't explain it," Robin says. "I know for certain that someone else was in my room, but if there was, they were gone now."

After using the bathroom and getting back into bed, an ordeal that took several minutes, Robin recalls that as soon as the room became dark once again, she suddenly felt another presence in the room with her.

"By this time, I was starting to freak out," she says. "I couldn't stop wondering if someone had broken in and was going to rob me or worse, maybe even kill me…. You just never know." If they were, Robin could do nothing about it. In her condition, she was totally vulnerable. She called out again.

"Okay, stop playing games. If you're going to do something, just do it."

No one answered.

"I'm not afraid of you," she said. "Go ahead and just get it over with. Do whatever you're going to do."

Suddenly, Robin says the darkness was shattered by the voice of a man that she did not recognize.

"You shouldn't be afraid, Robin," the masculine, yet soft, voice said to her. "I'm not here to harm you."

"Who are you?" Robin asked.

Silence. Then the voice again.

"I'm here to help you, Robin," the voice answered.

"Help me? How?"

"I'm here to tell you that even though you're suffering at present, you should know that you're not going through this alone."

"I'm not?"

"No, you're not. Your family and friends want to help.... I want to help."

"So, who are you?"

"I'm the one who's looking over you.... Don't be afraid. You're not alone."

As strange as it may seem, the idea that a strange man was in her room in the darkness with her and that she was totally vulnerable didn't really frighten Robin, even though she suggests that it would have been perfectly normal if she had been scared.

"What's your name?" she asked.

This time, there was no answer.

"Do you have a name?" she asked again.

When the voice did not respond this time, Robin pulled herself up in her bed and switched on the lamp again. To her amazement, she was alone.

Leaving the light on so she could see the mysterious man if he returned, Robin snuggled down in her bed with the covers pulled up to her chin and just lay awake for several hours. She recalled the words that her visitor had said to her and, suddenly, she felt better and more comfortable.

"It was the weirdest feeling," she says. "And I can't really explain it, but whoever this guy was, he made me feel better just by being there."

After that, Robin felt better about herself and more in control of her situation. Although she continued to struggle to understand why she had been inflicted with this dreadful illness, she was more at peace about having to live with its effects. Over the years, her symptoms have become progressively worse. She now has strong tremors, and most of the time she relies on a wheelchair to get around. She can walk with the aid of two canes, but she finds it difficult and is afraid that she might fall.

"And I'm afraid that if I end up on the ground, I might not get up," she says, displaying a surprisingly light attitude toward her condition, an attitude she directly attributes to her visitor that night several years ago.

"Whatever happened that night in my old apartment gave me a different perspective," Robin explains. "Somehow I came to understand that this was my life, and there was nothing I could do to change it…. I guess the simple answer is that I just found a way to accept it. I think that was the answer."

Since that time, Robin has had to give up her apartment and move back to live with her parents. She broke up with her boyfriend, but Jodie continues to remain at her side.

"Everyone has been so kind and helpful to me," Robin says. "My parents and Jodie have been very supportive, and even my old boyfriend keeps in touch. It's my fault that we broke up. He wanted to keep seeing me, but I didn't think it was fair to do that to him so I made him promise to find someone else, which he has, but he keeps in touch with me."

As to her visitor that night, Robin has no problem accepting that it was an angel.

"It was," she insists with conviction. "What else could it have been? I believe it was an angel, and it was sent to guide me through that terrible time in my life…. But whatever it was, it certainly made a difference in my life, and whatever quality I have now, I credit to my supportive family friends and to that visitor…to my angel."

The Messenger

ACCORDING TO THE CANADIAN CANCER Society, breast cancer is the most common cancer (excluding non-melanoma skin cancer) among Canadian women. In 2009, an estimated 22,700 women were diagnosed with breast cancer, and 5400 died of it. Every week, on average, 437 women in Canada are diagnosed with breast cancer and approximately 104 will die of the disease. One in nine women is expected to develop breast cancer during her lifetime, and one in 28 will die of it.

Vivian Younger, aged 46 and the mother of two, is one of those statistics, but she is determined to beat the dreaded disease. And she credits a most unusual experience for giving her the strength, courage and determination to rise to the challenge against the staggering odds.

It started around 2008, when Vivian was thinking that she should make an appointment for her regular mammography.

"I always worry about going to the doctor, so I tend to put it off. I know I shouldn't, but I do," she says, quickly adding that she understands having regular checkups and doing self-exams are important for every woman's health, and she does them at home.

"But I guess it's in my nature to worry. I suppose everyone does it, but my husband says I'm worse than most people he knows and sometimes calls me a hypochondriac, although hypochondriacs aren't known to avoid doctors, but I can't help it. That's just who I am."

Because she wasn't sick, Vivian wasn't really expecting bad news, but she has always gotten worked up whenever she has to see the doctor.

"I fret over it for weeks," she says, adding that sometimes she even has difficulty sleeping because she worries about it so much. "I know I drive my husband crazy when I get like that, and he finally tells me that either I have to make the appointment or he will make it for me. That always pushes me to do it."

It was during one of these cycles that Vivian had an unusual experience from which she finally accepted that angels do exist.

She was having an extremely restless night.

"I just couldn't get comfortable," she says, elaborating on the events. "I was tossing and turning, and I could tell that my husband was really getting frustrated with me. But try as I might, I couldn't force myself to fall asleep."

Finally, later into the night, she dosed off but wasn't sleeping all that well.

"It was one of those fitful sleeps where you're partially asleep but kind of half awake," Vivian says. "I just couldn't get relaxed. My mind was racing like it was going 50 miles an hour, but somehow, I drifted off. I think the last time

I checked the clock was around four o'clock, and since I usually get up at six, I remember thinking that I was going to feel crappy when I got up."

Regardless, somehow she dosed off, and she guesses that she had been sleeping for about half an hour, give or take a few minutes, when, suddenly, she woke up.

"You know how it feels when you're sleeping and you think you're falling?" Vivian asks. "Sometimes, it seems so real that you jump off the bed. That's what happened to me that night. I actually thought I was falling, and I remember grabbing hold of the bed as if it was really happening. I was startled, there's no doubt about that."

Once she realized that the falling sensation had only been a dream, Vivian managed to calm herself down, but that feeling of calmness lasted only a few seconds because what she saw next caused her even more concern. Nothing could have ever prepared her for what was about to happen.

"As I lay there thinking that I may as well get up because I knew I wouldn't ever get back to sleep, I suddenly got his strange feeling that somebody was watching me. I turned over to check on my husband to see if he was awake, but he was sound asleep," she recalls. "But I just couldn't shake the feeling. Then I thought maybe it was one of the kids, but I was sure they would have said something or come to the bed if they had needed me, so I told myself it wasn't either of them."

Suddenly, as she was trying to convince herself that there was no one there, the room filled with a brilliant flash of light that lasted only a second or two before it dispersed.

"It was kind of like the flash you see when a camera goes off," she recalls. "It was fast and then it became dark again. I had no idea where the light had come from, and I was starting to freak out."

Then the situation got even weirder.

"I swear that as I lay there, a man dressed in white with light brown hair down to his shoulders suddenly appeared at the side of the bed," Vivian says with conviction. "It was bizarre, and I started freaking out that there was a strange man in my house, but then this feeling of calmness came over me, and I knew this man meant me no harm. He didn't say anything, but I knew I had nothing to fear from him, whoever or whatever he was."

As Vivian watched, she eventually came to understand that this stranger in white had a message for her, and it was of the utmost importance.

"I don't know how I knew it, but I felt that this man was there to tell me to see my doctor as quickly as possible," Vivian says. "I'm not sure how I knew it, but this man was there to tell me that I had cancer."

And then, as suddenly as the mysterious visitor appeared, he was gone, but Vivian knew what she had to do.

"I won't lie. I was terrified by this," she says as the tears rush back to remind her of that moment when she realized that her life could be in danger. "I was crying and becoming so distraught that I had to wake up my husband. Naturally, he thought I had been dreaming."

But Vivian insists there was no way that what she had experienced could have been a dream.

"It couldn't have been," she says. "I was awake. I know I was, but my husband hadn't seen anything. Not that he would. He's such a sound sleeper that the house could fall down around him and he'd sleep through it, so I'm not surprised that he didn't see anything. But that doesn't mean it didn't happen.… I know that the man was there, and I just knew that he was a messenger sent to tell me that I could no longer put off going to the doctor."

Needless to say, Vivian couldn't fall back asleep.

"Sleep? Not a chance," she says.

Instead, she got up, made a pot of tea and sat looking out the dining room window until the sun finally came up and she had to get her children ready for school. Her husband again suggested that her experience was a dream, but Vivian told him it wasn't and that she knew for certain she had cancer.

"He told me I was crazy and that I was getting all worked up over a dream, but it wasn't a dream," she says. "It was a message for me. I couldn't feel the lump myself, but I knew I had breast cancer."

Later that morning Vivian phoned her doctor's office and made an appointment for a mammogram. She had to wait several weeks for an opening, but when she finally had the test, she had to wait for the results.

"The waiting was really hard for me, because even though I was certain it was going to confirm that I had cancer, I had no idea how bad it was going to be, so when they called and told me the mammogram showed an abnormality and that I needed to see the doctor, I didn't really freak out like I thought I would. I thanked the nurse for phoning and then I went about getting supper ready. It was weird, really. I always thought that I'd be a basket case if I ever found out that I had cancer, but I think once they told me something was wrong, I could finally come to grips with the reality. I knew I had cancer and I had to beat it."

Once she told her husband about the test results, he became emotional and apologized profusely for dismissing her vision as nothing more than a dream. From then on, he has been supportive and caring about her needs.

"He's been wonderful," she says. "I think it kind of weirded him out that things happened like they did. He did have a hard time coming to believe that a special messenger may have visited me, but he couldn't argue against the truth. The facts speak for themselves."

Following a series of tests, which included a biopsy, her worst fears were confirmed. It was cancer, but after surgery to remove two malignant lumps from her left breast and after several months of chemotherapy, Vivian says she feels stronger and healthier than she has felt for some time.

"It was tough going for a while," she continues. "And there were times when I didn't know how I was going to get through it, but with some wonderful doctors and nurses and very supportive family and friends, I've managed to move on to where the doctors have told me that I have a very good chance of a full recovery."

However, if the ordeal has taught her one thing, it's that no one should ever delay having regular checkups.

"No one is any more afraid of doctors than I was—still am, really—but I now know that checkups cannot be put off," she says.

Although some people have had difficulty accepting that an angel visited Vivian, she attributes her early intervention to that strange visitor.

"He was an angel, a messenger," she says, insisting that she understands some people find this type of stuff too far fetched to be real. "But I credit my health to whoever or whatever that visitor was. If that man had not showed up in my bedroom that night, I have no idea how long I would have kept putting off my visit to the doctor, and by the time I did get up the courage to go, it might have been too late."

So, Vivian adds, no matter what others believe, "I know it was an angel. I'm certain of that, and he saved my life."

PART V
Touched by an Angel

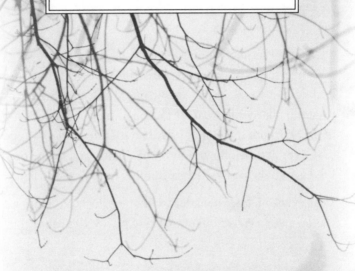

The Man in the Woods

ROBERT RANSFORD, WHO GREW UP IN rural Nova Scotia but now lives in Halifax, was just a youngster when he first heard the stories of his uncle's extraordinary experiences in the woods.

"Mother liked to tell the stories to me and my brothers and sisters, I think, to illustrate to us that no one walks alone on this earth," says the 76-year-old man who was raised in a strict religious family where such talk was in keeping with their lifestyle. "My mother and father vehemently believed in the teachings of the Bible, so I should not be surprised that she would tell us stories about angels and how they were sent to earth to help those in their hour of need."

Despite his advancing years and waning health, Robert recalls the stories in great detail. He says his family lived in different times with no computers or Internet or cell phones. Distractions, he calls them, adding that he grew up in a different era where children went outside to play or they hunted and fished.

"Mother could tell a good story, and maybe she put her own spin on them once in a while, I can't say for certain, but there's no doubt in my mind that from her perspective, everything she told us was the gospel," he says with sincerity. "Do I believe everything she told us? I don't know. Maybe some of it—most of it, I guess—but she certainly did, and who am I to say it wasn't true?"

One story in particular had a lasting impact on Robert. His mother's brother, his uncle Willard, became lost in the woods at the age of nine when he was out checking his rabbit snares. Robert's mother was two years older than Willard and so, at age 11, she retained vivid memories of what happened that December, many years ago.

"She insisted that she remembered the events just as they happened," he says, noting that his mother, who lived to be 83, remained sharp and lucid until the day she died. "She told us that it happened about a week before Christmas."

As the story goes, Robert begins, "She knew it was a Saturday because there was no school that day. My uncle went out in the woods around seven in the morning. My grandmother had told him to be home before lunch, and he always listened, or so my mother always said he did. When he had failed to return home by one o'clock, Mother said everyone in the house began to worry and panic. They knew it was not like my uncle to disobey his mother or for him to be late for a meal. When my grandfather arrived home a few hours later and my uncle still hadn't shown up, they knew there was a problem."

It was an extremely cold day and had been snowing heavily, so it would have been difficult traveling through the woods, even for grown men, but especially for a small boy such as Willard. With only a few hours of daylight remaining, Robert's grandfather quickly organized a search party of some of the neighborhood men and they set out to search for the missing boy.

"Mother says they were worried that something had happened to him," Robert says. "They feared the worst.

My uncle knew his way around the woods pretty well, so everyone just assumed that something terrible must have happened or he would have come home. They assumed he must have been injured or worse, maybe even dead."

With the snow coming down hard, searchers fanned out over the areas that the boy was known to frequent. "They knew they didn't have much time. If he was hurt and laying out there in the cold somewhere, then they needed to find him quickly. Perhaps it was already too late."

With Robert's grandmother and the other children remaining at home in case Willard came back, the men trudged through the deepening snow, searching for any clue that might lead them to the boy.

"Mother says they searched for hours but found nothing, and as the snow continued to come down, the men had to return home for fear that someone else might be lost," he says. "My grandmother was very distraught, my mother said. That would be natural, with one of her children missing in a blinding snowstorm."

Robert's grandmother didn't go to bed at all that night. Instead, she kept the lights on and a fire going in the kitchen stove with hopes that the lost boy might somehow find his way home. "She wanted to be there for him when he arrived," Robert says.

But Willard never came home that night, and by the next morning, the storm had dumped several feet of snow over the land.

"They said it was one of the worst storms they had seen in several winters," Robert says. "And because of that, everyone concluded that since my uncle was out there somewhere exposed to the elements, there was little chance that he could have survived. But Mother always said my grandmother was not having any of that talk in her house. She said she felt Willard was still alive, and she was not about to give up on him."

With the storm now passed and with the morning light upon them, Robert's grandfather and several of the men resumed their search, but they feared the worst. About an hour after the search party had left, Robert's grandmother, who was reportedly cooking a nice big stew so the men could have something warm to eat upon their return, heard a ruckus in the back mudroom. With the other children outside shoveling or playing in the snow, she thought one of them must have returned to the house for dry clothing or something.

"Who's there?" she called out from the kitchen.

"It's me, Momma," a boy yelled back.

Robert's grandmother was shocked and overwhelmed. She recognized Willard's voice right away. Entering the mudroom, she was relieved to see him standing there, all covered in snow and dripping wet.

"She quickly helped him out of his wet clothes and brought him into the kitchen beside the stove so he could get warm. Miraculously, my uncle was fine. There was not a mark on his body," Robert says.

How could that be, everyone wondered. How could a young boy survive 24 hours outside in the midst of a raging blizzard, one of the worst storms to hit Nova Scotia in years, and walk home unharmed?

"Apparently, when my uncle Willard realized the previous day that he was lost, he took shelter under a stand of dense spruce trees. But, as the storm got worse, he decided he needed to find some other place to hide, but by then it was getting dark and the snow was really getting deep. He didn't know where to go," Robert says.

"Suddenly, as my uncle told the story, there was a man there under the trees with him, and he told Willard to follow him. And he did. Willard insisted that he did not know or had ever seen the man before. They walked for what seemed like a long time, with the man continuing to urge him on through the deep snow. Finally, they came to a small opening—a crevasse, I guess—in a group of rocks, and the man told Willard to climb in there and to stay until the snow stopped. He would be safe there, he said."

Willard did as the stranger instructed and, hunkered down under some brush, he finally fell to sleep.

"The next morning, when my uncle woke up, the snow had stopped, and he decided it was time for him to come home, but he didn't know where he was or in which direction he should go. Suddenly, he heard a voice—the man's voice again—outside the hole that had been his hiding place, and that man told him to come out and to follow the rising sun."

He did as the stranger had directed, but it was tough going for the small boy through the deep snow.

"There were many times when he wanted to give up, but he said every time he felt like quitting, the man would be there beside him, telling him to keep going and reassuring him that he was almost home," Robert says.

"Finally, just when my uncle felt like he couldn't go any farther, he saw the smoke from the chimney at home, and he knew right away where he was. From there, the man told him he could go the rest of the way by himself, but that he should go quickly as his family was worried about him."

As word of the boy's miraculous survival story spread, everyone agreed he was fortunate to be alive because no one could understand how he had managed to stay alive in the freezing cold and driving snow.

"But beyond that, everyone wondered who this strange man was. No one seemed to recognize him from my uncle's description, and they never did find out the man's identity," Robert says.

"Furthermore, try as they might, no one could ever locate the grouping of rocks with the hole that had been my uncle's shelter for the night. He had been so turned around in the dense snow that he lost track of where he was, and he couldn't retrace his steps to that location ever again.… Of course, that only added to the mystery."

For the Ransford family, the return of the missing boy was a miracle, and Robert's grandmother immediately decided that the man had been an angel sent to earth to protect her son.

"In truth, the entire family believed that Willard had been blessed with the presence of an angel that had taken him to shelter and then had guided him home. My mother told us that her brother often spoke about the man in the woods, and he told them that even though he was alone, cold and lost, he never felt like he was in any danger. If angels do walk this earth, then my uncle Willard was one of the lucky ones, because it seems someone was walking beside him that night."

That Sinking Feeling

IF YOU BELIEVE IN MIRACLES, THEN you must believe in Rachael DeLong's story because she insists if not for the intervention of an angel some 70 years ago, she would not be alive today to tell the tale. And, she adds without hesitation, she believes it is her mission to spread the word of the Lord. She does that by sharing her experience with anyone who will listen.

Rachael's story began one humid August afternoon in northern Ontario when she was nine years old. She had gone swimming with her sister and their two older cousins. Although Rachel was the youngest of the group, she vividly recalls the events with great detail because, she explains, the life-altering experience forever changed her in ways that we cannot even imagine. To this day, she thanks God for giving her a second chance.

"I thank him," she explains, "because but for the grace of God go I.... When you look into the face of death and when the hand of God ultimately touches you, your life can never be the same. And that's what happened to me that day. Just as sure as I'm talking to you, I was rescued from certain death that afternoon, and from that moment on, I knew that there is a God and there is an afterlife and that he just wasn't ready to take me. I believe that when we leave this mortal life here on earth, we go to some place better, but on that day, I guess it wasn't time for me to go. I do believe that the Lord works in mysterious ways, and if he has a grand plan, then my role in that plan was that I was to remain here. I was given a second chance that day, and I like to think that I made the most of it."

It was so hot that day you could break out in a sweat just by standing still, Rachael recalls.

"It was the kind of oppressive heat that could make you feel ill," she explains. "For us kids, it was a good day to go for a swim. Now, we were all good swimmers and we were used to going to the lake without an adult. Perhaps we shouldn't have done that, and looking back now, I would never have allowed my children to go without me or their father being close by. But back in those days, people didn't seem to fear much, and kids seemed to be more carefree. Those were different times. Nowadays, you have to watch your children like a hawk. I don't think I would want to raise my kids all over again. We lived in a different world back then."

So on that day, then, it wasn't unusual that Rachael, her older sister and their cousins made their way to the little lake on the outskirts of the town where they lived.

"All the kids from town went there. We didn't even bother asking permission. We just did it. Thinking back now, I realized that we should have gotten our mother's permission to go that day, but when our cousins showed up and asked if we wanted to go to the lake with them, we just grabbed our swimsuits and towels and away we went without a care in the world. We were children. We didn't stop to think that what we were doing might be dangerous and that we should, at the very least, tell an adult where we were headed."

The walk to the lake took about 15 minutes, but to Rachael it seemed much longer because of the heat.

"It was sweltering, and we were hurrying so that we could get to the lake and get in the water. I'm sure that contributed to my overall state of exhaustion, but by the time we reached the lake, I was tired and I know I should have waited a few minutes before getting in the water so that I could regain my strength, but we were in a hurry, and you know how kids are. We never want to wait for anyone. So when we reached the lake, we just rushed directly into the crystal clear, cool water, and I still remember how it good it felt."

Unfortunately, the feelings of euphoria didn't last long, as Rachael was in trouble within minutes of entering the water. "There I was one minute, just splashing around and enjoying the cool freshness of the clear lake water when, all of a sudden, I'm down under the water and struggling to get to the surface."

To this day, Rachael has no idea what happened to her.

"I had been swimming in that lake hundreds of times so I knew where all the dangers were, and I was a good swimmer so there's no way I was in over my head," she insists. "But somehow I became confused and disoriented, and before I knew it, I was fighting for my life."

While Rachael struggled to keep from drowning, her sister and cousins, who had swum farther down the lake, had no idea the girl was in trouble.

"They were all older than me, and they'd often leave me behind as they went to the deeper water, which meant I was left alone closer to shore. Even though I was a good swimmer, I was afraid to go too far out. Normally, I stayed in an area where I could touch bottom with my toes, but on that day, I guess I ventured too far into the deep water because all of sudden I couldn't feel the rocks and soil with my toes. I guess I most likely panicked, and the more I struggled to get my footing, the farther out I floated. It was an awful feeling. I remember thinking that I was going to drown, and I could feel myself swallowing mouthfuls of water and starting to go limp. I may have been young, but it's true what they say about your life flashing before your eyes in the last moments just before death."

Rachael didn't know where her sister and cousins were. "Truthfully, I don't think they knew I was in serious trouble, and I was too weak to yell for them. Honestly, looking back on it, I don't think there would have been anything they could have done to save me, and I'm convinced that I was just about to die when all of a sudden, a pair hands reached down into the water, grabbed me under my arms and pulled me to the shore until I was close enough that I was laying on the sand. I don't know how long I was laying there, but it must have been several minutes before I started to come around. I will admit that I was disoriented when I opened my eyes and looked up into the sunshine, but I swear there was a man standing there looking down on me."

At first, Rachael was confused and frightened, but then the man spoke.

"His face was blocked out by the bright sunlight, so I really couldn't get a good look at him, but he talked in the softest, most mellow voice I had ever heard in my life. I can't explain it, but his voice was clear, and it sounded like music to my ears. He said, 'You will be safe now.' And then he was gone."

Rachael is sure that her rescuer was a man, but she didn't know where he had come from or where he went. "To this day, I have no idea who this strange man was, but he was there, of that I'm absolutely certain. How else did I get back to shore?" she asks. "I know I didn't swim there on my own strength."

And that's a valid question, one she has asked herself every day for the past 70 years.

"The only explanation I could come up with was that the stranger was an angel sent by God to save my life," she says with conviction, adding that she also asks why she was spared that day. "Why me? That's what I've asked my whole life, and I still don't have an answer, but whatever the reason was, I will confess that the experience stirred something deep within me that I had never felt before."

Having lost track of time after her brush with death, Rachael lay on the sand for several minutes before the others found her.

"'Did you see him?' I asked them when my sister and cousins finally came back to check on me," Rachael says.

"'See who?' they asked."

"'The man who saved me,' I said."

"'There's no one else around here,' they said. 'We didn't see any grownups.'"

Rachael pauses, then continues her story, "Now, I know I didn't imagine that this man was there, so I told them what had happened, and they just looked dumbfounded, insisting that no one else was around when they got to me. My sister explained that she became alarmed when she couldn't see me in the water, so they decided to come and check on me. When they did, they said they found me sprawled on the sand with half of my body still in the water and half—from the waist up—lying on the shore. My sister said that I was breathing but I wasn't conscious for several minutes, and one of my cousins was just getting ready to go for help when I started to come around."

Rachael was alarmed and even frightened when she first heard that the others had not seen the man who rescued her from certain death that day, but she quickly came to understand that what had happened to her was a miracle.

"The man was an angel," Rachael says emphatically. "There's no other explanation, and besides, there are too many questions that can't be answered. How did I get to shore? Why was I the only one to see the man? Why were there no footprints in the sand other than those that belonged to us kids? Where did he disappear to so quickly? Why didn't he stick around to make sure I was okay unless he already knew, and how could he know that unless he was an angel?"

The events of that day were forever embedded in that young girl's memory, and Rachael counts her blessings that whoever—or whatever—this man was, he came along at the right time. She's thankful he was there that day to pull her to safety.

"Was I drowning that day? Absolutely. Without a doubt. Another minute or two and I would've been a goner, but for some reason, God reached down and pulled me to safety."

Today, with three children and five grandchildren, Rachael has lived her life to its fullest.

"If I was spared from death that day to do something important, I hope I have done it," she says.

Rachael has a message from all of this.

"Never give up hope. Never stop believing. Life is precious, and miracles do happen. We just have to believe in them," she says with the utmost sincerity.

In the Nick of Time

OFTEN, WHEN WE SEE OR EXPERIENCE something so extraordinary that it defies a logical explanation, our first instinct is to deny that it actually happened. Laura Penny readily admits that's exactly what she did a few years ago when she came dangerously close to losing her four-year-old daughter, Lucy. She remembers the day as vividly as if it was yesterday, and it's a day she is never likely to forget.

It was just before Christmas 2006, and the day started when Laura, accompanied by her mother, Diane, and Lucy, went on a shopping excursion to Halifax, hoping to pick up some last-minute gifts.

"It was a Saturday, the last one before Christmas, and we knew it was going to be crazy in the stores. I wasn't sure I was going to go at first, but Mom insisted that we had to go and get our shopping finished as we were running out of time," Laura explains. "And she was right. Since I work during the week, I knew this trip would be my last chance to get to the city, so we planned to leave early and spend the entire day there."

It was business as usual for most of the day. They shopped all morning, had lunch and then shopped some more.

"We had a great morning, and like the good littler trooper that she was, Lucy tagged along without much fuss," she says.

"I've been taking Lucy shopping with me since she was born and she is usually very well behaved in the stores, but I think on this day she was overtired, and with the excitement and confusion connected with Christmas, by mid-afternoon, she was getting a little overwhelmed."

In hindsight, Laura realizes they should have gone home after lunch, but they were doing so well and knocking people off their lists that both she and her mother decided they should do as much as possible that day while they were already in the malls, and besides, they were running out of time.

"Honestly, we didn't even stop to think that maybe poor Lucy had had enough," Laura says. "I can't really fault her for what nearly happened when she had been such a little angel all morning long. I think we, as parents, sometimes forget that our children have needs as well and, in our haste, we sometimes overlook them, and I should have listened to her. I know she was tired and we should have just come home after lunch. Mom and I could have finished our shopping another time.… If anything would have happened to Lucy…"

It all happened so fast that Laura really didn't have time to react, let alone think about what was going on.

"Lucy was with me one minute, and the next minute she was gone," she says, the distress showing on her face and conveying the true terror of a parent who fully understands just how close she was to losing her precious daughter.

"She's always been an active and inquisitive child. Pretty much from the time she could make herself go across the floor, she was getting into things. And then, when she learned to walk, it was almost impossible to keep her pinned down. She's always been a mover, but she's always been good when we've been out. She usually stays right with me, and that's why it was such a surprise when she took off from me that day."

Laura became frantic when she realized that her four-year-old had suddenly left her side.

"If you're a parent and you realize that your child is missing, then you know what it feels like when you can't find them," she says. "To say I was panicked just doesn't seem to be the right word. I was terrified beyond belief that Lucy had gotten lost…or worse. You try not to jump to conclusions, but with everything that's going on in the world these days, it's impossible not to. I know how quickly tragedy can happen."

As Laura and her mother, loaded down with bags and parcels, made their way through the busy parking lot to the car, it suddenly dawned on Laura that Lucy was no longer with them. Laura had the car keys and had been walking ahead of Diane and Lucy. She assumed her mother had been keeping an eye on the child.

"But I guess Mom was distracted. I don't blame her because I know how easy it is to lose track of a child. When I realized Lucy wasn't with us, fear raced through me like a bullet," Laura says, as she relives the horror of that moment with vivid detail. "Whatever compelled her to wander off that day, I will never know, but as Mom and me threw our bags into the car and began looking for Lucy, I immediately thought the worst…. I just can't tell you how I felt. It was terrible, and I never ever want to feel that way again."

They immediately scoured the parking lot looking for the little girl and, by the time they spotted her, Lucy had wandered dangerously close to a bus stop. To make matters worse, a metro bus was heading in Lucy's direction.

"I'm not sure if the bus driver would have seen Lucy or not, or even if he could have stopped in time," Laura says, "but it looked to me like he was going to hit my daughter.... Something had caught her attention and she didn't notice the bus, but I'm not sure what it was that she saw."

Because Laura and Diane were too far from the bus stop to reach Lucy before the bus arrived, all Laura could do was yell for her daughter to get out of the way.

"I was just about crazy," she says. "Mom was yelling to Lucy to get out of the way, to watch out for the bus. I was running toward her, but it was like my legs were made of lead. They just didn't want to move.... I was certain that the bus was going to hit Lucy. She was standing right next to the curb where the bus stops, and I wasn't sure if the driver had seen her. I was freaking out, and all the while I was praying 'Please don't hurt my baby, please don't hurt my baby.'"

But just as it seemed certain that tragedy was about to strike the Penny family, a miracle occurred.

"Honestly, even after all these years, I still don't know what happened," Laura says. "I've relived that exact minute hundreds of times in my head since that day, but each time I think about it, I'm always left with more questions than answers.... It all happened so fast, but I thank God every day that Lucy was saved."

Recalling the events of that split second when Lucy was snatched from the clutches of certain death or at least serious injury, Laura says as she and Diane were running toward Lucy, a man suddenly appeared in front of the bus and quickly pulled her daughter to safety.

"I have no idea who he was or where he came from," Laura says, as the emotion rushes to the surface. "But out of nowhere, there he was, and he saved her.… One minute she was in the path of that approaching bus, the next minute she was standing on the curb. It was all a blur, but by the time I reached Lucy, the man was gone, and my daughter was fine."

As Laura and Diane embraced and hugged their little girl, Laura suddenly thought about the man—the hero—who had just saved Lucy from being hit by the bus. However, when she looked around for him, she couldn't find him.

"There is absolutely no way that any man could move that fast," she says. "But he was gone. Don't ask me how, but he had disappeared just as quickly as he appeared."

Laura says she stood there for several minutes searching the crowd of shoppers coming and going from the mall, but she could not locate the man.

"I owed him everything, and I wanted him to know how much I appreciated what he had done, but he was long gone," she says, adding that during the drive home and in the days that followed, she could not get the image out of her mind of that stranger darting in front of the bus and saving her daughter.

"In the end, I concluded that it was a miracle," she says. "I know what I saw, and Mom saw him too, but he moved so fast that she couldn't describe him if she had to, but we are both certain of what we saw. And Lucy saw him too. For a while, she told people about the man who pushed her when she was shopping with Mommy and Nanny, but we could never identify him. Lucy just didn't understand that that man may have saved her life."

Laura decided that the man must have been Lucy's guardian angel.

"So, yes, when people ask me if I really believe in angels, I tell them, yes, without question," she says. "If for no other reason than I'm certain that whoever saved Lucy that day was not human. But, no matter. Human or angel, that man saved my little girl, and for that I'm truly thankful."

The Passenger

IN 2008, THERE WERE 76 COLLISIONS in Nova Scotia that resulted in 83 fatalities. Ben Long believes that if not for an act of divine intervention that same year, his likely death would have inflated that statistic by at least one count.

Ben was alone in his car in early February, just before five-thirty in the morning. It was dark and frosty, the kind of weather that lends itself to treacherous road conditions. And even though the radio announcers were advising motorists to use extreme caution as there had been reports of black ice throughout the region, Ben pushed on at his normal speed.

"I knew better," he begins. "But you know, no one ever thinks something bad will ever happen to them. We just have this misconception that we are all indestructible or that we're immortal. But I have been driving these roads for many years, and I have seen some pretty stupid drivers, and some of them were doing some scary things that I always complain about, so I should have known better."

But the truth is that many drivers are just like Ben. They become careless and complacent.

Ben learned his lesson the hard way.

"So there I was, barreling down the highway, listening to the music and not really paying attention to what they were saying on the radio," he continues. "Stupid? Yes. Careless?

Yes. Dangerous? Absolutely, but I've been doing this for so long that I think I could make this commute with my eyes closed, and I admit that I got careless that morning.… It won't happen again."

About 20 minutes into the drive that morning, Ben began to notice that most of the other traffic on the highway was going painfully slow.

"Now…I'm one of those drivers who hates to get behind other vehicles if those drivers are going much too slow," he says. Although Ben knows you must be careful on the roads, overly cautious drivers can also be a traffic hazard, just as speeders can present a risk. "But I should have paid closer attention that morning. I can't argue with that."

But he was in a hurry, and whenever the opportunity presented itself, Ben passed whatever vehicles were in his way and continued on his journey.

"I was just cruising along when all of a sudden I realized that I no longer had control of my car," he recalls. He had hit a patch of black ice and the lost traction made the car skid. "Before I knew what was happening, the car was spinning out of control and I was heading straight into the path of another oncoming vehicle."

It was at that moment that Ben's outlook on life changed forever…but in a good way.

"We've all heard that when you're facing possible death, your life flashes in front of your eyes," he continues. "Now, I'm not saying that's what happened that morning, but let's just say I experienced something that changed me forever."

Ben's first instinct when his car started sliding into the opposing lane of traffic was to hit the brakes and try to steer his car toward the ditch.

"But I hit a patch of ice and had lost all control of the car," he recalls. He was becoming frantic as he realized that another vehicle was in the other lane, and he knew that if he crossed the yellow line, it was likely that he would hit the car head-on. "God knows how that would have ended."

Realizing the danger he was in and understanding what was about to happen, Ben struggled with the steering wheel, but it wouldn't respond.

"The car had a mind of its own," he says, "and I thought I was a goner. I remember thinking that this was it.... I was going to hit that other car and maybe kill myself and God knows how many other people along with me. All I could do was sit there.... I tried to straighten [the car] out, but I couldn't."

As his car swerved across the centerline and headed directly into the opposing traffic, Ben thought about his wife and children and wondered how they would cope with the news of the accident.

"I wasn't really worried about myself," he says. "I was thinking about my family and about them getting a call telling them that I was just killed. I can't imagine what that would have been like for them.... I know my wife would have lost it."

Obviously, it didn't come to that.

Ben explains that once he accepted that he couldn't control the vehicle, he let go of the wheel and braced for the resulting impact. And he hoped the driver in the other vehicle was bracing as well, because it seemed a crash was imminent.

"I knew there was nothing I could do about what was about to happen," he says. "All I could do was go with it and hope, somehow, we would survive."

It was at that moment, as his car continued to slide directly into the path of the approaching vehicle, that he discovered he no longer was alone.

"It all happened quickly, and I was freaking out, so I admit that my mind may have been playing tricks on me, but I swear there was another man sitting beside me in the passenger seat," Ben says with conviction. "Now I may have been losing it, that's true, but I also know that when I left my yard that morning, I was totally alone in my car. If there was someone else with me, then I have no idea where he came from."

He was stunned.

"Just imagine how you would feel.... You're about to have a head-on collision and you know you could die, and then, all of a sudden, there's this stranger sitting beside you who appears out of thin air," he says. "It causes my head to hurt when I think about it. I actually thought that maybe that man's sudden appearance was proof that I was going to die. When you start seeing visions like that, what else would you think?"

As the car slid, Ben tried to remain calm, but the man didn't say or do anything.

"He just sat there in the seat and looked straight ahead at the road," he says. "He was as still as a statue, and he didn't say a word."

Before he knew what was happening, Ben's car was swerving past the approaching vehicle, coming to rest on the opposite shoulder of the road.

"We were so close—only inches apart, really—that I could have reached out and touched the other car when we passed. Don't even ask how I missed that car," he says. "I have no idea, but I can tell you that it was a close call…really close, and I know I should have hit it. It's a miracle that I missed it."

When his car came to a stop, Ben just sat there.

"I couldn't move," he says. "I was literally frozen in my seat, and my heart was beating so fast that I thought it was going to burst out of my chest."

When Ben turned to look at the passenger seat where his mysterious companion had been only minutes earlier, there was no one there.

"So here I am, after coming within inches of a serious crash in which I probably would have died, and all I can think about was this stranger," Ben says, pausing as if reflecting on just how close he came to dying that morning.

"I admit, it really did freak me out. Truthfully, I was spooked, and I couldn't figure out how or why this would have happened. I was sure I was going to hit that other car, yet here I was, and the other car kept going on its way. The driver didn't even stop."

Any logical explanation for what exactly happened in his car that morning has eluded Ben in the time since the near mishap, but he believes something beyond this world intervened and saved his life.

"Why that would happen, I have no idea," he admits. But Ben believes he must have been spared for a reason.

"Maybe there's some sort of major plan for all of us, and maybe it's as simple as 'it just wasn't my time,'" he suggests. "But whatever the reason, I was just happy and thankful that I could go home to my family that day."

As for the man in the passenger seat, Ben can see no logical explanation for what he saw, but he wonders if it was an angel.

"What else would it have been?" he asks, adding that he appreciates many people have difficulty accepting such a possibility. "I have a hard time accepting it myself, but something extraordinary happened in my car, and now I just stop questioning it. Whatever happened, happened, but I'm truly thankful that I'm still here, whatever the reason."

Wonders in the Woods

WHEN JUDY TURNER, 58, WAS A CHILD growing up in rural Nova Scotia, she heard many fascinating stories about the wonders in the woods. Her grandfather, a farmer and woodsman, had worked the land with great pride and dedication, and Judy says that he seemed to have a unique bond with the earth. He truly respected the land, which, in turn, gave up its rich bounty to him—but he had to work for it. She describes him as being a true outdoorsman.

"He was a fantastic old man," Judy fondly remembers. "He worked hard in his vegetable gardens and out in the woods, and it was clear to me, as a child, that he loved being outside with nature. He had a strong work ethic, but then again, most of the people from the older generation never shied away from hard work. They understood that their survival and that of their families depended on them getting the job done, not like today's younger generations with their attitudes of entitlement."

But that's another story.

Judy remembers her grandfather, Wilson Turner, as a large, burly man with a thick black beard and hands the size of a baseball catcher's glove. She describes him as a gruff man—the kind of man you wouldn't necessarily think would be good around small children. But, she immediately adds, "He had a huge heart, and no matter how busy he was doing his chores, he always had time for us kids whenever we'd visit the farm."

Judy chuckles when recalling those days 50-some years ago when he'd actually get the children to help out with the chores.

"He'd always ask, 'How would you like to help Grampy?' And we'd always jump at the chance to do whatever we could for him," Judy says as a broad smile crosses her face while talking about the old man. "I suppose it was his way of getting some free labor for a few hours, but I didn't care what he wanted me to do. I loved being with him, and I'd follow him into the gardens to help him dig potatoes or I'd help him stack the wood or clean out the cow poop or collect eggs from the henhouse. I'd spend hours with him, and he'd talk to me just like I was a grown-up, and I loved every minute of it…. They are great memories."

One characteristic about her grandfather stands out most in Judy's memories.

"He respected us kids," she says. "He never talked down to us. He treated us like adults, and even though I was really young, I could sense that he was sincere in his approach to dealing with people…. He was such a wonderful man. It was a sad day for me when he died."

But she's getting ahead of the story.

During those many visits to the farm, Judy learned all about the wonders in the woods. Her grandfather regaled the children with fantastic stories of extraordinary experiences he'd had during his many years of working in the forests, first in northern New Brunswick, where he grew up, and then in Nova Scotia, where he settled with his wife and four children.

"I suppose there's a chance that some of it was embellished somewhat to impress us kids," Judy admits. "He certainly could tell a good story, but he always insisted that everything happened just as he said it did. And to me, it really didn't matter. I loved to listen to him talk about his experiences in the woods because he added little details that made his stories come to life."

These stories kept her enthralled for hours. One specific story that he often told always gave Judy goose bumps and left her feeling inspired and enlightened even though, in truth, it really was one of tragedy.

Wilson began working in the lumber camps of the dense forests of northern New Brunswick when he was 15, and he worked there for about 12 years. During that time, he had had many close calls, but none were more urgent than the one that occurred just after his 20th birthday.

"He worked in the lumber camps up there and he said he liked it, but it was hard, especially in winter when the snow was nearly up to your waist," she says. When the snow got too deep, the men often had to shut down operations and close up the camps until conditions improved in the spring.

"It had been snowing hard for several days, and they knew that the camps would soon have to shut down for a while until the harsh weather passed," she explains. "It was in the afternoon, just before dark, and the snow was really coming down. Grampy and another guy—I don't know his name—decided they would work until the light was gone because they wanted to get as much wood as possible so they could meet their quota before the snow forced them to stop," says Judy.

Because of the snow, most of the men had left the woods and returned to camp, but Wilson and this other man pushed on, going over a ridge where they hoped to make a fresh cut. Even though that area had not yet been fully surveyed and marked out, the two men thought they would get a start there.

"He said it was tough going," Judy recalls. "The snow was getting deeper by the minute, and they knew they should have gone back to camp instead of going farther into the woods, but when you're being paid for the amount of timber you cut, you just don't give up easily.… Not Grampy anyway, so the two men pushed on, fully aware that with the amount of snow coming down, their trail would almost immediately be lost. But they were experienced lumbermen, and they believed they could find their way back.… But they weren't counting on someone else having to come find them. As it turns out, deciding to continue to cut timber was a tactical error that almost cost Judy's grandfather his life.

Locating a fresh stand of virgin timber, the two men found a big tree and went to work. With two experienced foresters on the job, Judy's grandfather had told her that they could fell a tree in 15 to 20 minutes…providing they didn't run into trouble. However, no matter how prepared or experienced a forester may be, accidents can occur, and they often did in the thick, dense forests.

"He had great respect for the forest and the trees, but sometimes things just happen, and on that day, Grampy and the other guy seriously miscalculated the amount of snow that had fallen," Judy says. "With the two of them working on the tree, they made quick progress and had it coming down in about 10 minutes. However, just as the tree started to fall, the upper branches became wedged up in the canopy and wouldn't budge. That's when the men made a serious miscalculation, and Grampy always wished that they had left the tree alone and walked away, but that meant they'd lose whatever they would have earned from that tree. And in those days, they just couldn't afford to do that. So, even though they may have known better, the men went to work trying to pry the tree free of its upper branches, and within minutes, the large timber came crashing down to the ground…. By the time they realized what was about to happen, it was too late for them to escape and…both men were trapped under the enormous weight of the snow-covered branches."

Judy pauses to catch her breath. As she recalls the words of her grandfather, it's almost as if she has transported herself to that time and place and is reliving the impact of the large timber crashing down on top of the two men.

"Grampy said by the time he came to, it was pitch black and he couldn't see a thing," Judy begins again. "He quickly called out to the other guy, but his friend didn't respond…. He kept calling, but the other guy didn't answer…and he never would, because when the tree came down, several of the larger branches went right through him and he died instantly. But Grampy didn't know that. He kept hoping that since he wasn't dead, maybe his friend was alive as well."

Wilson was trapped under the weight of the branches and was seriously injured. His legs were pinned, and he could tell his right leg was broken pretty bad. He was also bleeding from his head where a branch had bashed him and knocked him unconscious for a while.

"No matter how hard he struggled to get free, Grampy was not able to get out from under the tree," Judy continues again. "I can't imagine what that would be like…. Being hurt and being trapped under the weight of that tree, not being able to move. And, to make matters worse, it was snowing harder than before the accident, and Grampy knew that if he didn't die from his injuries he would most likely freeze to death out there in the darkness, and he was still fretting over his friend. But that would be him, though. No matter how bad he might be hurting, Grampy would be thinking about the other guy first."

Judy's grandfather knew the other men back at the camp would eventually realize that he and his friend had not returned, but he also realized that in such a bad snowstorm and in the darkness, they wouldn't begin a search until the next morning when it got light again. They would not risk losing anyone else. There was a rule of the forest—never put a man in harm's way, even to save another. And to make matters worse, the searchers wouldn't know where to look as the two men had gone over a ridge that had not yet been marked for cutting.

"So he feared they wouldn't look in that area because they weren't supposed to be there," she says. "As the hours passed, Grampy could feel the coldness starting to take over his body, and no matter how hard he struggled, he just couldn't get free. He always said that he was about to give up and that he accepted that he would die out there in the forest trapped under that tree in the middle of a blinding snowstorm. It wasn't good, he said. He really thought the end was near."

But it wasn't meant to be.

"Grampy knew that he could die, and…he had come to accept the inevitable. He told us kids that he had come to peace with it," Judy says matter-of-factly. "He said he knew he was at God's mercy and that if it was the plan that he was supposed to die, then so be it. He said that's when he noticed he had company."

Judy pauses again, taking a deep a breath, then continues.

"He was alone, except for the friend who couldn't respond, but Grampy suddenly noticed that another man was there with him. Although he didn't say anything to my grandfather, the man stood beside Grampy as if guarding him," Judy says. "Grampy admits that he was in pretty bad shape, but he is certain that he was not seeing things. He said that when this man appeared, he got a strange sensation in his body and suddenly felt warm all over.… Grampy had lost a lot of blood, he was in shock and it was snowing pretty hard, so he should have been freezing, but he insisted that he was suddenly warm."

As Wilson lay on the cold, wet ground in the dark, severely injured, he believed he would somehow come through this.

"If he lived, there's no doubt it would be a miracle," Judy observes, adding, "Grampy had faith that this man was his savior or his guardian angel sent to protect him and, despite his predicament, he remained calm for the remainder of the night. Years later, when he told us this story, Grampy insisted this was no ordinary man and that he could tell his life was going to be spared."

The man, who never spoke and whom Wilson could not describe because it was dark, remained with him for several hours. When daylight broke, Wilson suddenly realized the mysterious man had vanished just as quickly as he had appeared. And, in another positive development, it had stopped snowing. He knew it wouldn't be long until the other men from the camp found them. Although he didn't know for sure that his friend had been killed, Wilson concluded that the other man was dead. Still unable to move, Wilson's only course of action was to lie there until he was found.

It took several hours, but eventually he could hear the voices of men as they moved through the woods, calling out the two men's names. Mustering enough energy to call back, Wilson feebly yelled out to his rescuers, who quickly located him and his deceased friend.

"Gramps always felt really bad about the other guy," Judy says. "Somehow, I think he blamed himself for what had happened, though there's no way they could have foreseen the tragedy. He insisted that they had taken all the necessary precautions, but sometimes accidents just happen, and there is nothing we can do about that. I think, in time, Grampy may have come to forgive himself, but he always knew how fortunate he was to have survived that ordeal."

Wilson also told his family that it was more than luck.

"Grampy believed a miracle had taken place out there in the woods that night," Judy says. "When he got back to the camp and was able to talk to a couple of the men who had rescued him, he asked if they had noticed any other foot-prints in the snow that morning. They told him no. The snow was fresh and unbroken. They told Grampy it didn't appear that there had been anyone walking around there since the night before when the tree came down. But there was, Grampy said. It's just that whoever that man was didn't leave footprints, and that was just another one of those wonders in the woods."

PART VI
In Angels We Trust

But for the Grace of God

IN AUGUST 2005, HURRICANE KATRINA hit the southern coast of the United States with devastating and deadly force. It was reported that more than 1800 people lost their lives and over $100 billion in damages were left in its wake. But for Margaret Millwood, the killer storm left something greater behind—it left a legacy of humility and appreciation for life, as well as a renewed spirituality.

Hurricane Katrina formed over the Bahamas on August 23, 2005, and subsequently crossed southern Florida as a moderate Category 1 hurricane, causing death and flooding in that state before strengthening rapidly in the Gulf of Mexico. The storm weakened before making its second landfall as a Category 3 storm on the morning of Monday, August 29, in southeast Louisiana, but it was still packing a severe punch. It caused major destruction along the Gulf Coast from central Florida to Texas, much of it the result of the storm surge.

The most serious loss of life and property damage occurred in New Orleans, Louisiana, which flooded as the levee system catastrophically failed, in many cases hours after the storm had moved inland. Eventually, 80 percent of the city and large tracks of neighboring parishes became flooded, and the floodwaters lingered for weeks, making rescue virtually impossible.

And if not for a message from her guardian angel, the 48-year-old Margaret says she would have been right smack-dab in the middle of the disaster and she may have even been killed.

"It started with a dream," she recalls, explaining that she had been planning a trip to New Orleans from her home in the Maritimes to visit her friend, Paula, whom she had not seen for almost seven years. "At first, I was really excited about the trip. I had been planning and saving for it for a long time, and…I was really excited about rekindling our friendship."

However, about a month before her scheduled departure date, Margaret's feelings of excitement and exhilaration changed to those of apprehension and fear and even dread.

The two women were nurses and had worked together in the local hospital for five years until Paula moved south with her husband and eventually ended up settling in New Orleans, where he worked in the construction business and she in a residential care facility.

"We were really close," Margaret explains, adding that their relationship was more like sisters than friends. "We just had this special bond. We were together all the time, and I had a really difficult time when Paula left. Losing my close friend was like losing one of my arms. I was devastated."

While the two women remained in touch through letters, phone calls and the Internet, their plans to physically reunite at least once a year were always scuttled by some unforeseen circumstances. For Margaret, the delay was usually connected to a lack of funds.

"It's expensive to travel, and it's not like I have extra money just laying around," she says, adding that she and her husband, Bill, struggle to make ends meet, meaning large expenses such as a major trip were rare.

"I was going to be staying with Paula and her husband so accommodations were not going to be a problem, but I still figured it was going to cost me about $3000 for my plane ticket and the spending money that I figured I needed. Paula told me not to worry about anything, but you just can't go on a trip like that and skimp, and I didn't want to be a burden on her. If I was going, I was going to have a good time, and I needed money for that to happen."

Margaret saved money for several years and finally was able to scrape up enough money to make the trip a reality.

"I was so excited and pumped about seeing Paula again," Margaret says. "I had missed her so much. It was going to be great. She had lots of activities planned for us to do while I was there. Since I had never been to New Orleans, she wanted to make sure I got to all the hot spots, but honestly, for me, it was more important that I spend the time with her. It didn't matter to me if we just hung out at her house. As long as we could get caught up with each other and spend time together, then everything else was secondary."

As the date for her trip grew closer, Margaret became more excited about the prospects of reconnecting with her best friend. But in July 2005, about a month before her departure, that excitement turned to apprehension.

"It started as a dream I had one Sunday night after I had talked to Paula on the phone," she begins. "We were going over some last-minute details about the trip. Paula is really good at making travel plans, and she wanted to make sure everything went off without a hitch."

All seemed normal when Margaret went to bed that evening, but shortly after midnight, she suddenly woke up in a cold sweat after having what she describes as a disturbing and vivid dream.

"It was one of the most unusual dreams I think I've ever had. It didn't feel like a normal dream; it felt so real," she recalls. "In the dream, I could hear and see it raining, and the wind was blowing really hard. I didn't know where this storm was, but I could tell I was in a city somewhere. This lasted for a few minutes, and then, all of a sudden, out of nowhere, there was this massive rushing of water everywhere, and I got the strange sensation that I was drowning. The feeling was so strong that when I woke up, I felt like I couldn't breathe."

At first, Margaret didn't think much about the dream, believing it was some sort of anxiety about her upcoming trip. She had been working extra shifts at the hospital to pick up some additional cash, so she thought that being overworked, combined with the excitement of planning a major trip, probably contributed to her stress.

"I didn't even bother to tell my husband about the first dream, but when I had the same dream again the next night, I began to think that something wasn't right," Margaret says. When she told Bill, he, too, thought it was most likely stress related. He suggested that she take a relaxant before going to bed so she could get a good night's sleep. "And that worked. I slept really well that night."

Margaret doesn't remember dreaming at all. However, as a nurse, she understands the dangers associated with becoming dependant on such medication, so she chose not to take a pill the next evening. To her relief, the dream didn't come back.

In fact, she didn't dream for three nights, and Margaret was beginning to think that all was well again. However, that was not the case. On the next night, the dream returned, and it returned with a vengeance.

"When I woke up, I was terrified," she says. "I even cried and trembled so hard that I shook the whole bed and woke up my husband, who is normally a very sound sleeper. Bill told me that if the dreams were going to get to me like that, then I should see a doctor. Of course, I told him I didn't need to see a doctor, that it was just a dream, but deep down inside, I knew it was more than that. It didn't feel like any other dream I had before."

With the dreams returning every night, and Margaret continuing to reject the pills, she wasn't getting much rest, and her body was beginning to get rundown.

"I was exhausted, dead tired," she says. "So finally I did talk to one of the doctors at the hospital where I worked, and he said the dreams were most likely anxiety related. He asked if I was afraid of flying, and I told him that while I didn't like it, I managed to convince myself that it was something I had to do if I wanted to travel. I had flown several times in the past, and although it made me nervous to do so, I didn't remember it causing me that much anxiety. But the doctor said sometimes the mind can play tricks, especially when there's added stress, say, from a fear of flying or worrying over money, both of which could have been contributing factors in my case."

The doctor prescribed Margaret some mild sedatives, which he assured her were harmless. They would help her rest, he said, but weren't strong enough that she would develop an addiction.

"And they helped, and I slept well again," she says.

It was now two weeks since the night of the first dream and still two weeks away from the day of her departure, and although Margaret was anticipating the trip, she also had an overwhelming sense of foreboding. It felt as if a huge storm cloud was hanging over her.

"It seemed to get worse every day, and I was beginning to think I was going crazy," she says. It was about this time that she had the weirdest experience in her life.

"I had just gotten off the night shift and had gone straight to bed when I got home," Margaret says. "I dozed off, and I don't think I was asleep for any more than 10, maybe 15, minutes when I heard the woman's voice."

Because she was home alone, the realization that she had just heard a voice scared Margaret beyond belief.

"I was terrified. The kids were in school and Bill was at work, so I knew there was no one else in the house with me. I thought, this is it, Margaret, you're really losing it. I know it was a woman's voice, but since I was asleep when I heard it the first time, I wasn't able to understand what it had said and that frightened me even more."

She didn't know what to do, so she lay there with the blankets pulled up tightly to her chin, hoping that whatever the voice was, she wouldn't hear it again.... But she did, and this time she understood the words.

"I heard it," Margaret insists, "just as clear as day.... The woman told me not to go to New Orleans. That was it. No explanation or anything. She simply said, 'Don't come to New Orleans.'"

For Margaret, that didn't seem like an option, because she had planned this trip for months, and all the arrangements were made. There was no way she could cancel now. Besides, she desperately wanted to see Paula again.

But over the next two days, as she thought about the voice she had heard and as the message sank in, she began thinking that the woman and the dreams were a warning to her. She didn't understand what was happening, but she eventually concluded that something was trying to tell her to stay away from New Orleans.

"I didn't know why, but I began thinking that I should not take this trip," Margaret says. "I knew people would think I was crazy to cancel at the last minute, but I had this growing feeling in the pit of stomach that all this was a warning. As much as I wanted to take this trip and as much as I wanted to see Paula again, I just couldn't stop thinking that I shouldn't go."

She became so convinced that her dreams and the voice were a warning that she contacted the airlines to ask about canceling her ticket. When she found out her travel insurance covered sickness, she talked to the doctor at the hospital again to see if she would qualify, and she did. The doctor said that if the trip was bothering her that much and was affecting her health, he would help her fill out the necessary paperwork.

"I really wanted to take this trip, but I was becoming fanatical about it," she says. "My husband thought I was crazy, and while Paula said she understood, I know she was very disappointed in me. She didn't say it, but I know she was upset with me. I felt really bad about what I was doing, but I had to do it. It was as if I was compelled to stay away from New Orleans. It took a lot of paperwork, and I incurred a penalty for canceling my flight, but I know now that all that happened for a reason."

Later that month, as she watched news reports starting to come in about the massive hurricane bearing down on New Orleans, Margaret came to understand what the dreams and the woman's warning meant.

"I know someone was telling me to stay away from that place because of that storm," she says, "and I believe it was my guardian angel. It was a terrible, terrible tragedy.... So many people were killed and left homeless that it makes my problems look pretty minor, but obviously I was glad I didn't go to New Orleans because, if I had, I would've been there right at the exact time that the storm struck. When I think about what could have happened, it just gives me goose bumps."

As Hurricane Katrina took aim on New Orleans, Margaret had great concern for her friend Paula and her family. "I prayed to God that they would be okay," she says. "There were a few tense days when I lost contact with Paula, but when she finally called and told me that she and her family were fine, I was so relieved that all I could do was cry. Their home suffered some damage but nothing major, and they weren't hurt.… They were the lucky ones."

As Margaret thinks back over the events of that summer, she is even more convinced that an angel had contacted her with a warning not to travel to New Orleans. "As crazy as I know it sounds to some people, this happened to me for a reason. I have no idea what would have happened if I had taken the trip, but for some reason, I wasn't supposed to go. When we talk about it now, Bill and Paula agree that something unusual was happening to me, but they stop short of acknowledging that it was an angel or divine intervention. But I know that's what it was, and considering what happened down there, I'm thankful that I took the warning to heart."

In the end, Hurricane Katrina went down in the history books as the costliest hurricane, as well as one of the five deadliest, in the United States. Among recorded Atlantic hurricanes, it was the sixth strongest overall. Years later, thousands of displaced residents in Mississippi and Louisiana were still living in trailers.

As for Margaret and Paula, they were reunited the following summer when her friend returned to the Maritimes.

The Woman Wore White

I*T'S A LONG-HELD SUPERSTITION IN THE* fishing communities and rural out ports of Atlantic Canada that it's bad luck to bring a woman onboard a ship. While modern-day sailors may have long ago dismissed such old wives' tales, some traditional seamen continue to follow the old ways, fearing that it's better to err on the side of caution than to tempt fate.

Ronny Wolfe is one of those seasoned fishermen who believe it's better to follow the traditions of his forefathers than to turn his back on the generations of fishermen who came before him. And Ronny has good reason to honor those who sailed on the rugged, often unforgiving waters of the Atlantic Ocean long before he was born almost 70 years ago.

Without so much as a second's hesitation, he says that it was one of those old ways that saved his life.

"It was about 15 years go," Ronny says. "I don't really care what other people think. I know what I saw and that's that…. I saw an angel, and it's for that reason that I'm still alive to talk about it."

Ronny has been going to sea since he was 13 years old, and, growing up in a fishing village, he has heard all the superstitions about the sea and the warnings that bring on bad luck—whistling on the deck of a boat, wearing black on a boat, having people with red hair onboard, starting a journey on a Friday, stepping onto a boat with your left foot first, looking back once the ship has left port, or saying the words "drowned" or "pig" while you're at sea.

However, taking a woman onboard a boat was considered the ultimate in bad-luck omens.

"I've gone out on the boats a long time," Ronny says, "and I knew a lot of fellows who wouldn't sail if there was a woman onboard. They would just as soon miss a trip as be out there with a woman. It just wasn't something you did back then, and I grew up listening to those old guys, so I went along with it."

Even to this day, if he was still fishing, it's unlikely that Ronny would venture to sea if a woman were onboard his boat. He believes to do so would be like tempting fate and inviting a tragedy, and even though it might be considered old-fashioned to believe in such superstitions, he would still follow that tradition.

"I've seen too many things when I was out to sea," he says. "And I've seen too many men go down that I figure why bring bad luck onto yourself if you don't have to."

So it was with this philosophy that he went down to the wharf one November morning some 15 years ago to help stock the boat and get it ready for their trip the next day when lobster season opened. Ronny became extremely agitated and worried when he saw a woman on the deck of the boat with one of the other crewmembers.

"I had pretty much retired from fishing by that time," he says, adding that he was going along on opening day as a favor to the captain, a man whom he had known and respected for many years. "He needed someone with experience to help out, and I agreed to help out for the first few days until the rush slowed down."

Traditionally, the opening day of the fall season on the Atlantic is a hectic one as the fishermen head to the rich lobster grounds off the coast. If the weather doesn't cooperate or if the fishermen are careless, it's also often a time of great tragedy as boats capsize and sink, and men are lost.

"When you're going out there on the rough seas in some really bad weather, you really don't need any more bad luck," Ronny observes, adding that there's usually more than a sufficient number of problems to tempt fate. He admits to being a superstitious person, and he adds, "It worked for me. I don't really care what other people do. I'm only worried about me and my fellow crewmembers. I always considered us lucky to go out and come back alive. Fishing is a good life, but it's a hard one, too, and you earn every cent you make…. And you're always at the mercy of the weather."

And although he made a good living from the sea, Ronny also knows that he was lucky to work for more than 60 years on the ocean and escape with his life. Many others were not so fortunate.

"But don't get me wrong," he says. "There were a couple of close calls…some closer than I care to admit, but that's the life of a fisherman. You take the risk because you have to. My father was a fisherman, his father was a fisherman, and his father ahead of him was a fisherman, so I always knew that I would be a fisherman, too. It was just meant to be. And it was an honest living."

However, while Ronny credits his safety record to careful planning and always being prepared for every possible problem, he also believes an element of luck was involved.

"You just don't work on the waters for all those years and walk away at the end of that time without considering yourself lucky," he says, adding that's the reason he believes in a lot of those old ways. "Because if you follow them, they will save your life."

Considering everything that he had learned from his decades of fishing and working on the water, as well as from growing up in a superstitious family, he knew right away that something was wrong.

"We had two young guys with us, but the captain was an old hand," Ronny recalls. "There's no way that he would have a woman on his boat. He's kind of old-fashioned that way, just like me."

However, as Ronny approached the boat, he could see the woman was near the stern.

"I couldn't really see her face because I was too far away, but I could tell it was a woman, and I could see that she was wearing something white," he says, pausing to regroup. "But I knew there was something strange about the whole situation right from the minute I laid eyes on her. I just got this strange feeling in my gut, and I knew it was a warning.... And I admit that it scared me."

Ronny had heard many stories about fishermen seeing angels on their boats just before an accident happened, but he had never seen one himself.

"But I know that's what I saw that morning, and I'm glad that I paid attention to the warning," he says. By the time he reached the boat that was tethered at the end of the wharf, the woman in white was gone. "She just disappeared, just like that," he says, snapping his fingers for emphasis.

Ronny asked the captain and the two other crewmembers if they knew who the woman was, but they had no idea what he was talking about and insisted no one else was onboard. When he described to the other men what he had seen, the captain quickly became alarmed, but the two other men shrugged it off and dismissed it as foolishness.

"I'm sure they thought I was a crazy old man," Ronny observes with a shrug of his shoulders. "But I had gone through a lot and seen a lot of strange stuff in my life at sea, and I wasn't about to let two young punks get the best of me. I told them what it meant for a woman to be onboard a boat, especially when it was a woman in white like the one I had just seen. I also told the captain that he could go out the next day if he wanted to, but I wouldn't be going with him. It was a sign that something bad was going to happen on that boat and, as much I wanted to help the captain, I couldn't bring myself to go out.... I just didn't feel right.... And he understood that."

Ronny Wolfe had managed to survive his many years working in the fishing industry largely by paying attention to his intuition, and in this particular case he felt compelled to remain on shore.

"I knew the captain really well, and I knew what I had seen had spooked him too, but he couldn't just cancel his trip," Ronny says. "Lobster fishing was his bread and butter, and he had to go out. I knew he was worried, but he had no other choice."

A lot of fishermen will throw caution to the wind on the chance that these old wives' tales are nothing more than superstition and will still go to sea.

"They have bills and other obligations, so they can't just decide to stay home whenever they want," Ronny says. "And there was no way this guy could miss the first day of the lobster season, so he planned to leave the next morning, with or without me."

Ronny remained at the boat for the day helping the crew prepare to depart the next morning, but he had decided that he wouldn't sail with them.

"I knew they'd be one man short," he says, "but I also knew that the captain wouldn't have any problems picking up an extra man if he still wanted one, because there's usually a lot of guys hanging around the docks looking to pick up a trip or two. I was only going along as an extra anyway, so the captain didn't really need me."

As it was, the captain decided that he didn't require the fourth set of hands.

The following morning as the boats, laden down with their lobster traps, left the port, Ronny watched from the shore. As a cold, damp wind blew in off the water, he could not get the image of the woman in white out of his mind, nor could he stop thinking that it was a warning of impending tragedy.

"I know it sounds crazy, but I was certain that something bad was going to happen," he says, shaking his head. "But you gotta do what you gotta do, and fishermen take chances all the time."

As the boats steamed out of sight, Ronny made his way back home, where he set about doing some chores in his woodshed.

"It's not unusual for me to spend hours there," he says. "I love working with the wood, and I get lost in there, and that means I lose track of time. That day, I didn't even bother coming out for lunch. I had no idea what was happening until my wife came in and told me."

When Ronny heard that two boats had been swamped not too far from the coast, he immediately recalled the woman in white he had seen the previous morning.

"I knew it had been a warning," he insists, adding that he's convinced the woman in white had been an angel sent to warn him that he shouldn't go out on that boat. "I know it's hard for some people to believe this stuff, but I believe it, and I'm glad I do. If I hadn't paid attention to that warning, God knows what would have happened.... I might not be here today."

Even 15 years later, Ronny still gets goose bumps when he recalls the image of that woman on the deck that morning. "I get chills," he says.

He was thankful to hear later in the afternoon that the captain and one of the two crewmembers had been rescued by the Coast Guard. Sadly, a second crewmember was lost, along with the boat.

"It was a tragedy," Ronny observes, reflecting on the events of that day. "I know the captain had a hard time dealing with it. Fishermen take risks all the time, and a lot of men are lost because of it. When that happens, the whole community feels it. It was a terrible thing that the young fellow died that day. I knew his family really well, and he was a hardworking man. It was a big loss for them, and they took it hard…. I'm not sure his mother ever recovered."

Although Ronny admits he has no idea what might have become of him had he gone on the boat that November day, he is convinced an angel had come to warn him that his life might be in danger.

"For some reason, someone didn't want me to go out on that trip, and I'm glad I listened," he says. "But you know, those beliefs come from a long way back, and we pass them on to our children for a reason. In this case, I was thankful for the warning, and I'm just happy that I recognized it for what it really was."

About the Author

Vernon Oickle

Vernon Oickle was born in Liverpool, Nova Scotia, where he still lives with his wife and two sons. He has 30 years experience in the weekly newspaper business and has won numerous awards for writing and photography. In addition to his busy writing schedule, Vernon is past president of the Atlantic Community Newspapers Association, chairman of the local school advisory council and chairman of the committee to refurbish the old burial ground in Liverpool. He also lectures on various aspects of newspapering, including investigative reporting, writing and newspaper design, and he has been a political commentator for local radio and cable television. He is editor of the *Bridgewater Bulletin* and the author of 10 books, including *Disasters of Atlantic Canada* for Folklore Publishing.